AN AGENDA FOR

CHANGE

AN AGENDA FOR

CHANGE

A GLOBAL CALL FOR SPIRITUAL AND SOCIAL TRANSFORMATION

JOEL EDWARDS

GENERAL DIRECTOR OF EVANGELICAL ALLIANCE

ZONDERVAN.com/
AUTHORTRACKER
follow your favorite authors

 **ZONDERVAN®**

An Agenda for Change
International Trade Paper Edition Copyright © 2008 by Joel Edwards

Requests for information should be addressed to:
Zondervan, Grand Rapids, Michigan 49530

ISBN-13: 978-0-310-28371-3
ISBN-10: 0-310-28371-x

All Scripture quotations, unless otherwise indicated, are taken from the Today's New International Version®. TNIV®. Copyright © 2001, 2005 by International Bible Society. Used by permission of Zondervan. All rights reserved.

Some Scripture quotations are from The Word on the Street. Copyright © 2003, 2004 by Rob Lacey. Published by Zondervan, Grand Rapids, Michigan 49530.

Internet addresses (websites, blogs, etc.) and telephone numbers printed in this book are offered as a resource to you. These are not intended in any way to be or imply an endorsement on the part of Zondervan, nor do we vouch for the content of these sites and numbers for the life of this book.

Joel Edwards asserts his moral right to be identified as the author of this work.

Interior design by Melissa Elenbaas

Printed in the United States of America

08 09 10 11 12 13 14 • 10 9 8 7 6 5 4 3 2 1

CONTENTS

Acknowledgements   7

Preface: Background Noise or a Great
Transforming Enterprise?   9

PART ONE:
Presenting Christ Credibly to the Twenty-First Century

1   Will the Real Jesus Step Forward?   17

2   Christ Among the Gods   25

3   Rumours of Angels   33

4   Christ the Conversationalist   41

5   Rock Steady   49

PART TWO:
Rehabilitating "Evangelical" as Good News

6   What's in a Name?   57

7   A Good Time to Be Good (News)   65

8   To the Left   71

9   To the Right   77

10   To the Centre   85

11   A Good News Afterthought   93

PART THREE:
Engaging in Spiritual and Social Transformation

12 God's Gone Public   99

13 Towards Evangelical Citizens   105

14 In for the Long Haul   111

    Questions for Discussion and Response   119

    Notes   129

    About the Author   137

ACKNOWLEDGEMENTS

This conversation began as pool-side soliloquy whilst I was on vacation in 2004.

Having given a lot of thought over the previous ten years to what it means to be involved in leadership of an evangelical movement, it seemed to me that I had an obligation and privilege to do three things: to present Christ credibly; to remind evangelicals that, by definition, Christians are good-news people with a calling to affect the spiritual and social fabric of the nation; and to reassert to non-Christians that very same message.

As everybody knows, talking to yourself in public is bad for one's own credibility. So I am indebted to all of my colleagues and Council members in the Evangelical Alliance UK who joined in the conversation and agreed that it should be encapsulated in our mission statement. But I am also obligated to so many friends from other parts of the world who fed in their perspectives as the conversation grew. In this regard, special thanks to Geoff Tunnicliffe, international director of the World Evangelical Alliance, whose passion for these issues ignited my own thinking from time to time.

Writing a manuscript is one thing, getting it to this point is quite another. So very special thanks to Mike Morris, Helen

Calder and the good folks at Zondervan. Their support and encouragement have been invaluable, and their collective belief in the work was so firm it caused me to read it again! My sincere hope is that the conversation continues beyond that which has been captured in these pages.

And finally, a very special thanks to colleagues who spared me the task of doing the important details. I shall forever be indebted to my executive assistant, Vikki McLachlan, whose commitment and devotion to duty often makes me appear better than I really am. And last but by no means least – much, much gratitude to Ian Wedd, whose writing skills and support are inestimable.

If this conversation turns out to be profitable to the evangelical church, perhaps I'll go on vacation more often.

—Joel Edwards
August 2007

BACKGROUND NOISE OR A
GREAT TRANSFORMING ENTERPRISE?

Last night I finished watching season six of the American television political drama series *The West Wing*. The episode ended with the new emerging Democratic presidential nominee giving a powerful speech to party conference delegates about their responsibility to choose a candidate who would represent the core values they held in their hearts. It was riveting stuff; I played the speech four times. But the address wasn't just heard by the party faithful. Everybody interested in the race for power was watching – including the opposition.

What is fascinating about modern political party speeches is that they have become megaphones to the wider world. They are addressed to cynics and enthusiasts alike.

In a similar way I have a primary audience. My "party conference", so to speak, is the growing evangelical family across the globe. But I am also hoping that this short book gets picked up by Christians everywhere who wish to be part of the great unfolding Christian story. The story of the church sent out to advance the kingdom of God, not with a defensive posture but as servants of transforming good news.

If you live in the global west or north it is difficult any longer to think of the Christian church as a great transforming enterprise, and for very good reasons. Christian faith in Europe, and even to some extent in America, has lost most of its political control. The Christian values by which the west was won have been gradually eroded. In Whitehall, Brussels and the White House, Christians can no longer make assumptions about laws being based on Christian principles. Europe has been described as "a continent in search of its soul"[1] and Britain is going through cultural convulsions, a kind of spiritual schizophrenia. As I often say, Britain is like a man with a tattoo which says "I love Jane". The only problem is that Jane left him thirty years ago and he's just not sure what to do with the tattoo. Or as Cardinal Murphy-O'Connor has suggested, Christianity has become background noise in British culture.[2]

In all of this, church attendance is plummeting. Having to address a press conference in the year 2000 to tell everyone that over 2.8 million people had left our churches in the previous twenty years was not a particularly joyful moment.[3] Nor was describing the dark shadow which looms over the church's future up to 2040, including the statistic that only 6 percent of our children currently have any live links with the Christian church. No doubt most of us reading this in America, Europe or New Zealand (described as the most secular country in the world) will be able to add to the gloomy statistics.

But there is good news too. Thankfully, God is not Euro- or US-centric. Those of us who struggle to see growth may look in awe – or holy envy! – at the explosion of churches in Africa, Asia, Latin America and parts of eastern Europe. We can draw confidence for the western context from what God is doing elsewhere in the world.

And God is also at work in the midst of our western desperation. Old denominations and young movements alike are undergoing structural reviews. Visions and missions have been overhauled. Sacred cows have been dragged to the altar of modernisation. Fresh expressions of faith, emerging churches, new experiments in evangelism, and even painful discussions about the atonement are all part of an active and vibrant Christianity, wrestling to impregnate the culture with good news. It's agonisingly bewildering, but it's a pain we must embrace.

In fact, if your church or organisation has not known major change in this period of fermentation then it's possible your momentum has already stopped and a slow death is taking place.

Faced as we are with an array of challenges, what is to be done?

First, it is absolutely critical that Christians remember that the church is premised on Christ.[4] We must know that Christian faith is both durable and sustainable. Our future will not be determined by the nature of our relationship with post-modernity but by our relationship with Jesus. Nothing will change in the fortunes of our nations unless we are first transformed by the renewing work of the Spirit who renews everything.

Secondly, we are called to be like the "men of Isaachar who understood the times and knew what Israel should do".[5] The German pilots who flew over Dover during World War II were extremely skilful and courageous, but military historians say they lost the battle partially because they had no idea what the radar instruments they were looking at actually did! Intelligence-led spirituality is called for. We need to know the terrain in which we are called to serve. Being good preachers with big congregations, which come in from the cold and love to listen to us, just isn't good enough anymore. In western nations which have lost their Christian scruples, effective ministry will no longer be measured by our skills in the pulpit but

12

by our ability to nurture and equip our people to chase away the darkness and change the nation.

Thirdly, we need to ensure that we are wearing the right equipment for the new terrain. Fighting desert battles in winter relief will lead to disaster. Sermons, strategies and attitudes which work on the basis that western society is still actively or nominally Christian are not just ineffectual, they are a downright hindrance. Effective and transforming ministry will recognise that although our nations may still have the institutional structures of godliness, they are ones which generally now deny God any real authority.[6]

> In western nations which have lost their Christian scruples, effective ministry will no longer be measured by our skills in the pulpit but by our ability to nurture and equip our people to chase away the darkness and change the nation.

In setting out to write *An Agenda for Change,* I chatted with prominent leaders across the world who allowed me to draw from the archives of their personal wisdom, scholarship and experience. A key piece of advice I was glad to hear was that we had no need of an exhaustive academic work on this subject. Much has already been written. This, then, is something else. It is more the beginning of a conversation. My hope is that it will remind us of a few truths we already know and perhaps raise some provocative new ideas to consider. In September 2005, the Evangelical Alliance UK devoted its entire Council meeting to these issues, and I am hugely in their debt for allowing me to hijack the proceedings while they pretended not to notice.

In brief my arguement is this: biblical witness is not called to tip-toe through the twenty-first century. It is meant to transform society. It will do so by presenting Christ credibly to the culture. For evangelicals this means reclaiming the idea that we are good news, called to a long-term vision for spiritual and social change.

The three sections can be treated as stand-alone discussions, but really the entire book is a single conversation. A conversation about an *agenda for change*.

PART 1

PRESENTING CHRIST CREDIBLY TO THE TWENTY-FIRST CENTURY

> *"What's the gossip?*
> *What are people saying about me?*
> *They worked it out yet?"*
> —Matt 16:13 (The Word on the Street)

For two thousand years the Christian church has been talking about Jesus. It has written thousands of books and preached a trillion sermons and populated countless seminars. In spite of this, the vast majority of modern Christians work with cultural misconceptions about Christ. This is due in part to poor teaching and in part to the paucity of biblical awareness about who Jesus really is. As we will discuss later, there is an urgent need for a *biblicised* church.

Our Christian ignorance consequently means that people "outside" the church also have no real idea who the authentic Jesus is. We have given them an incomplete version. We have busied ourselves with conversations between ourselves, but when all is said and done, our culture knows little other than a dumbed-down Jesus.

This means that the understanding our neighbours have of our faith is often based on TV caricatures of Christians, or on their contacts with our absolute attitudes, woolly convictions, check-list religion or occasional bouts of relevance. If you go to church, then you may just occasionally stumble across the fully presented Christ. If you don't, your chances of doing so are pretty limited.

And this is tough on Christ because his credibility stands or falls on our reputation. This is the divine risk which God took. A king is a king, but if it's not too irreligious to say so, in any battle a king is only as good as his army. If I were God, I would be far more bothered about Christians than I would be about what secular newspaper commentators might be saying about me.

But I'm not God.

Christ is already credible because God has said so.[1] But apart from a church which fully understands this truth, how will the twenty-first century ever know it? This is our great task. And when this task becomes our greatest joy and foremost preoccupation, many more people will know just how credible he has always been.

WILL THE REAL JESUS STEP FORWARD?

When Martin Scorsese's film *The Last Temptation of Christ* came to our screens, most of us missed the point. The outcries of blasphemy we sent up were all reactions to the scenes of Jesus abandoning the cross, having sex with Mary Magdalene and settling down to family life. But if Jesus really was fully human, as we believe, then those were reasonable temptations he would have wrestled with. If there was any blasphemy it had a lot more to do with the scenes depicting him as a disorientated miracle worker with an identity crisis.

For if there was one thing Jesus was clear about it was who he was. By the tender age of twelve he was already consumed with his Father's business.[1] Over and above his miracles and teachings, Jesus was passionate about his identity. Nothing mattered more to him than the intimate awareness of who he was and the unique mission which flowed from this.

When he did a brief public opinion survey in the gospels, it was in the shadow of Caesarea Philippi where Greek mythology, Roman religion and Hebrew legends met. And so his question about his identity really was a hard one to answer. But it was designed to provoke Peter's outburst declaring him to be God's Messiah.[2] The disciple's remark was an echo of what John the baptiser had said some time before,[3] what God himself confirmed[4] and what the apostles would go on to say again and again.[5]

But while Jesus may have been clear about who he was, his followers ever since have generally had more problems. Because apart from God, who can fully know Christ? Within a short period after Peter's great confession it was evident that even he himself had failed to grasp precisely what it meant for Jesus to be the Messiah.[6] And if Peter couldn't fathom his own statement, we should not be surprised that everybody else has struggled to understand it since. In the earliest letters of the Christian church, Paul – the most prolific of the Bible writers – devoted more material than any of his contemporaries trying to help us understand just who this Jesus is.[7]

From its inception the Christian church has stumbled through heresies, factions and councils to describe how it was possible for one person to be truly God and truly man: frail but not fallen. The church had to wrestle its way towards orthodoxy with what we now know as the Apostles' Creed, and, like Peter's confession, the words did not come easily.

But a knowledge of the real Jesus is essential, not just for Christians but for wider society, because his influence is so wide. The reality of an individual who has set the western calendar, permeated human thought and history for over two thousand years, and influenced the culture of the dominant nations for a millennium demands to be taken seriously. The huge questions about just who Jesus is are more than mere theological musings.

And getting Jesus right is also vital because those who claim to follow him do so much in his name.

When they get his identity wrong, we see the cruelty of the Crusades, the Inquisitions and entrenched political conservatism. When they get it right, they are inspired to lead sociopolitical campaigns, battle slavery and establish humanitarian services. This Jesus turns out to be far more at home in the issues affecting communities than he is in ivory towers or church politics.

And though secularists once dreamed that by now he would be fading into the obscurity of primitive superstition, Jesus has proved irresistibly resilient. His followers simply will not go away and his words won't fade. Outlawed in twentieth-century Albania, Russia and China, Christians there have re-emerged in the twenty-first century with greater force, talking incessantly about him. He is culturally adaptable but never captivated by any one culture. In Africa, Latin America, eastern Europe or Northern Ireland, his followers emerge as critical prophets against the status quo. Properly heard and understood, there has always been something revolutionary about his claims – not only about himself but about what it means to be human. As New Testament scholar D. A. Carson reminds us, the gospel is always "subverting and overthrowing the categories of culture".[8]

> Jesus is culturally adaptable but never captivated by any one culture.

And Jesus' words are far-reaching. If in fact it is true that he is the only way to God, then other religions are implicated. If God will only save us because of Jesus,[9] then every individual is obliged to accept or reject that claim. If Jesus is real, everyone is drawn into conversation with him. We only escape that conversation if we can satisfy our intellect that Jesus as the son of God was simply imagined by a handful of Jewish folk two thousand years ago and remains the great delusion of more than two billion people alive today.

So this explains why theologians have worked so hard to respond to Jesus' question: "Who do people say that I am?" And it explains why there has been so much intelligent debate about the *historic Jesus* over against a *Christ of faith*. In other words, some scholars say we have to differentiate between the real and historic Jesus as opposed to the "myths" about him in the gospels, and the Jesus figure we understand only by our faith which makes him real to us.[10]

Although evangelicals may have little patience with unorthodox portraits of Jesus, we must at least concede that it has always been difficult to answer the identity question. Those who claimed he was Elijah, one of the prophets, or even John the Baptist were as far off the mark as anyone in modern times who would equate him with John Wesley, D. L. Moody or Billy Graham! The truth is that nobody has the last word on Christ.

But we don't throw up our hands in despair. We keep looking in order to discover and re-discover the real Jesus. For how else will he be presented credibly to our world? Understanding his true identity is vital both for a healthy church and effective mission. In fact, it's often the desire to reconnect good news to our world that has driven so many writers to dig beneath the debris of the westernised church,[11] in order to reread Jesus' words against his own culture so that we might relate them more powerfully to ours.

And we can approach the scriptures with a confidence that they have stood up to the interrogation of better minds than the average thinking Christian. Evangelical scholarship has thrown off its monkey suit and escaped from the circus of academic ridicule to stand confidently beside its liberal counterpart. There is no intellectual embarrassment in taking the gospel portraits of Jesus seriously.

So what of the real Jesus?

First and foremost we must embrace the fact that he was fully human. Matthew is keen to present him as "Jesus the Messiah the son of David".[12] The Word made flesh[13] is a deliberate starting point. But he was also perfectly God in human form. Any portrait which loses this balanced mystery is a forgery. In this dual reality Jesus was totally convinced that he was the same as God.[14] This was why the desert temptations which preceded his ministry were focused so keenly on his identity. His greatest temptation was not to turn stones to bread or even to worship the devil; it was to doubt his true identity. Had he given way on that issue, his entire ministry would have been undermined.

> Jesus' greatest temptation was not to turn stones to bread or even to worship the devil; it was to doubt his true identity. Had he given way on that issue, his entire ministry would have been undermined.

The real Jesus was also a teacher and, more than any other title, he liked to think of himself as "Rabbi". Not that his teachings were straightforward. Nothing could be further from the truth. Not everyone got his words about the kingdom, and often the secret of his message ensured that only the really keen were likely to get it. And he didn't spend too much time on the small issues. In the main, his teachings were big-screen stories about the kingdom. He was a storyteller, not a systematic doctrinal technician. At no point in his ministry did he attempt to give a literalist historical overview of Old Testament passages, as did Stephen or the writer to the Hebrews.[15] Instead, stories poured out of him and into the lives of his followers as they walked together or sat on the Galilean hills.

And there can't be too many of us who have failed to notice that the real Jesus seldom gave the ordinary people a hard time. He reserved his anger and frustration for the religious rulers and authorities. He spent time with the poor and marginalised. He healed their sick, fed their multitudes, dragged them from ignorance and blessed their children. He loved sinners, taught and touched the poor, and socialised with prostitutes. Jesus was not risk-averse; he was always in love with the outlaws.

The Christ of the scriptures was ruthlessly impatient with the hypocrisy in established religion but this did not make him a liberal; he still believed in future judgement. And although always quite clear that he was the only way to God, he was also clear that the kingdom was far more generous than people assumed – a great mustard tree in which all types of birds could rest. Even on the cross an undeserving thief was waved into paradise as a result of his desperate faith in Jesus.

How then has this life-giving and utterly generous Christ become so unrecognisably domesticated by evangelicals? How have we presented him as so risk-averse and timid that we often marginalise him from the people he came to live and die for?

Our sin, it seems, is that we have clothed him so heavily in our likeness that he has become discredited in our culture. Few people have an opportunity to say "no" to the real Jesus. The one they have rejected is the bad imitation we have offered.

Few people have an opportunity to say "no" to the real Jesus. The one they have rejected is the bad imitation we have offered. It's like giving someone a poor quality cappuccino from a dispensing machine rather than a freshly made cup from an Italian coffee shop.

It's like giving someone a poor quality cappuccino from a dispensing machine rather than a freshly made cup from an Italian coffee shop.

The real Christ was always willing to touch the untouchables. He reached out to those of other faiths and cultures. He healed the ones who did not return to thank him. He allowed a prostitute to wash his feet in public. And when he taught, it was never predictable or moralising. All the people said that they had never heard anything like it before.

The real Christ turned the most ordinary water into the finest of wines.

CHRIST AMONG THE GODS

In one week during October 2006, a massive front-page dispute was provoked by a British cabinet minister who invited Muslim women to remove their veils in his private constituency meetings.[1] In the same week a Muslim police officer created controversy because he was excused from duty outside the Israeli embassy, and Fiona Bruce, a BBC journalist, was criticised for wearing a crucifix during a news broadcast.

Just a few days earlier a *Daily Mirror* journalist had asked my views on the role of religion in society. He wanted to know if faith was a friend or foe.

We are living, it seems, in an age full of the challenges presented by the world's diversity. The political agenda has changed our conversations about faith. Talk of ecumenism is old hat; the new debate is about inter-faith dialogue. It is now virtually impossible to find any community insulated from discussions about religion. Christians can talk all they want about doctrine and truth, but actually, as far as our society is concerned, our credibility and acceptability now depends on our willingness to present ourselves as having a different faith rather than a superior idea.

For the past three decades the world has been playing cultural musical chairs as populations have migrated across boundaries and different traditions. Not only are we crisscrossing the globe, but there seems to be very little time to settle before new developments send us off once again into increasingly complicated spirals of international relationships. We are now in the global village, where the great religions have come to political prominence in ways we could not have imagined one hundred or even fifty years ago.

It's not just that religions are growing. They are now growing in close proximity to each other. In the mid-nineties I used to hear a lot about "comparative religion". That now feels like a very old idea that suited the academic mind-sets of those who studied other people who lived "somewhere else". Today's world is far smaller. It has thrown religions together. Ideas about identity, faith and nationality are now part of one big global discussion. It's much harder to be "comparative" when faced with an American Muslim who works in the stock exchange and lives next door, or the Hindu shopkeeper in Birmingham who sells you a daily newspaper written in French. If you pick up a phone in New York to call your American bank (which is facing a Spanish takeover), you could actually be talking to someone in India.

All of this means that there is a constant community obligation to be conscious of other cultures. And it also means that anything which smacks of cultural imperialism is unacceptable. America struggles with its international profile precisely for this reason. And in the context of Palestine, Bosnia, Rwanda and Northern Ireland, we are all on the lookout for settings in which religious claims have fostered brutally enforced ideas of cultural superiority.

This is precisely what Dr Jonathan Sacks, the Chief Rabbi of Britain and the Commonwealth, was worried about when he wrote his excellent and controversial book, *The Dignity of Difference*. Dr Sacks' position accurately reflects a good deal of contemporary thinking about the tyranny of difference. "If I am right, you are wrong. If what I believe is the truth," he surmises, "then your belief which differs from mine must be an error which must be converted, cured or saved. From this flowed some of the great crimes of history."[2] And so our current social systems have grown to celebrate difference. They hate superiority with a post-modern passion.

The economic and global pressures which have merged political differences in the last decade are now pressing in on religion, insisting on a religious "sameness" to mirror the cultural climate. Our primary service to the political agenda, it seems, is not to believe but to sanitise and play down our differences.

All of this means that the politics of community relationships is only comfortable with faith if it is entirely inclusive. Once exclusive claims are attached to our devotions or social action, our faith becomes suspect. "Exclusive" will now be read as "fundamental" or "extreme".

In the constellations of the gods, Jesus is allowed to be different – even uniquely different. But he is not allowed to be better and certainly not superior. If Jesus has any supremacy it must be limited to Christians. He is not allowed to claim it over anyone else. Christians who claim that Jesus is "above" other deities can expect to be politically outlawed.

> Once exclusive claims are attached to our devotions or social action, our faith becomes suspect. "Exclusive" will now be read as "fundamental" or "extreme".

How on earth, then, can our Christ be presented credibly to this kind of world? Let me offer four possible suggestions.

First, Christians confuse themselves by assuming that there is something strange about the contemporary western pluralist position. For the first three hundred years of the church's life it was a perfectly normal challenge to have to present Christ credibly in a multi-faith and hostile environment. For centuries that has also been the reality for much of the non-western church.

Western Christians have been spoilt by the privileges of Christendom.

In the new religious reality, presenting Christ credibly has a lot to do with discovering the courage to believe he is who he said he is. He presented himself as uniquely God's son[3] – supremely different in every respect – and the early church believed that salvation came only through his death and resurrection.[4] It is all or nothing. Christ is either Lord over all or nothing at all – and countless Christians have been persecuted for saying so. It may well now be our turn.

The liberalism in Christian faith which mushroomed in the twentieth century attempted to present a credible Christ by muzzling this idea. But Christ was never made credible by people apologizing for the claim that he is God. This claim remains an enduring strength of growing evangelicalism and the Achilles' heel of a "liberal" Christian tradition which appears to be ebbing away.

Embarrassingly, the stigma of his cross is integral to his credibility.[5] God does not thank us if we blunt the point. A church which dumbs down the lordship of Christ is on "a route to suicide".[6]

Somehow, Christians have come to believe that we have no moral right to say that "Jesus is Lord" over all. The political developments which have called into question our right to say so are the early stages of a problem that is potentially going to get worse. In our thoughts many of us have given up that freedom, at least beyond the safety of our pulpits. But if our

> The claim that Christ is God remains an enduring strength of growing evangelicalism and the Achilles' heel of a "liberal" Christian tradition which appears to be ebbing away.

liberal democracy has any legitimacy, then our right to say that "Jesus is Lord" should be undiminished. Others may disagree with us, but in order for pluralism to make sense, we should be allowed to say what we believe. Christian faith must now put liberalism, freedom of speech and religious liberty to the test; we must ask the twenty-first century for the right to say what we believe – so long as we refuse to denigrate another person's right to believe something else.

Christians should be free to say that "Jesus is Lord" – even if society has to humour us in the process. Our value as citizens should then be judged not by what we say about Jesus but by our acts of kindness, which serve everyone indiscriminately.

Secondly, if we believe that Christ is "Lord of all", the credibility of such a claim only really counts when we offer it with humility and respect for others.[7] Jesus never bragged about his divine sonship. At the age of twelve he was even fairly matter of fact about it.[8] When he was baptised and declared to be God's son, he immediately went into forty days of obscurity.[9] Even demons were muzzled from advertising his identity.[10] Jesus' credibility was never dependent on an aggressive defence of his name or nature but on the self-effacing silence of his authority. As Brian McLaren suggests, there is something quite compelling about the mystery in his message which turns out to make it far more powerful.[11]

Jesus is Lord not because Christians say so but because he is. His lordship is not a truncheon with which to beat other people; it's a biblical truth best understood when offered with as much humility as we can muster. Christians who believe that gratuitous offensiveness against other gods is a mark of Christian witness should make a special note: Paul did not rubbish the goddess Diana.[12] As Chris Wright has argued, the early church was intelligently flexible in how it presented Christ to the Gentiles as opposed to the Jews.[13]

Our primary calling is not to put down other people's gods. It is to lift up Jesus Christ.

> Jesus' lordship is not a truncheon with which to beat other people; it's a biblical truth best understood when offered with as much humility as we can muster.

Thirdly, we present Christ credibly by letting him speak for himself. The great temptation for Christians fearing the loss of power and influence in society is to politicise Jesus in the public square. Christians deserve to be heard, we say, because, in the west at least, we have been the majority faith for many centuries. We begin to sound as churlish as teenagers arguing for the best seats in the theatre because daddy owns it. And so our encounters in the public square become defensive ones.

Added to that is the fact that the foremost concerns we have taken to the lobbying halls and the public debates have all been associated with the defence of specific agendas: sex, marriage and morality. These agendas are important, but our ability to defend them is declining. So what people are likely to hear is a Jesus solely concerned with sex, abortion, marriage, gambling and the like. Ask any discerning member of the public, and this is likely to be the Christian agenda they best recognise.

But if Jesus was allowed to speak for himself, this would not necessarily be the agenda on which he would hang his credibility. Whether we like it or not, he did not have a great deal to say about homosexuality and was quite selective about sex-talk. What he really wanted to talk about is best summarised in his very powerful manifesto: freedom of captives, the opening of blind eyes, and liberty for the oppressed.[14] What might it cost us to be immediately identified with such an agenda? In a world with overcrowded prisons, millions of addicts, an epidemic of HIV/AIDS and unprecedented levels of people trafficking, Christ could be far more credible than we have allowed him to be.

Instead we have gagged him with sex-talk. We have not allowed him to speak out against the corruption of our powerful institutions or to challenge religious hypocrisy.[15] We have not allowed our world to know just how highly he thought of children or how eager he was to be the best servant the world had ever seen. People don't know that he weeps over the city and cries when his friends die.

Fourthly, Christ will be credible if we are convincing about what makes him so unique in relation to other gods.

As incomprehensible as it may be, born of a virgin he is the only one who claims to be truly God and fully human.[16] We will have to find the courage to tell people we believe something we can't fully explain. And what's more, this same Jesus lived in time and space. He has no credibility as a mythological figure. His historicity is as central as his teachings and miracles. If he did not live as a first-century Jew in Palestine, he would cease to be credible.

> Christ will be credible if we are convincing about what makes him so unique in relation to other gods.

But Jesus is also unique in his claims to forgive people, from paralytics to adulterers, foreigners to convicted thieves. He assumed the freedom to forgive. He is the only Saviour who never delegated forgiveness to God. And he is the only one who claimed that this power to forgive multitudes was made possible by his death and resurrection. His claims to be God's son and predictions of his resurrection – which ironically contributed to his death – mark him out amongst the gods. His credibility depended on it.[17]

And there's more. Having been revealed in space and time, he said he would return to earth in the full regalia of glory. Two thousand years later we are still required to believe him.

At every turn, the things which are uniquely Christ leave us no room to compromise. It's not just that he has given us hard things to believe or a penetrating moral philosophy to live by. Others have also done that. It is not just that he makes moral demands which stretch our lifestyles beyond our comfort zones. He is unique because he calls us into the unbelievable. Jesus is credible in part because everything about him is incredulous, and only people who follow him where other gods have not gone will discover precisely how credible he is.

It's all quite stupendous. Faith in Christ defies our senses whilst elevating our minds. What makes Christ credible is this: this foolishness about him is precisely the raw material with which faith in Christ is built. And he does it so that when people put their trust in him, he alone gets the credit.

RUMOURS OF ANGELS

I am a classical Pentecostal. I grew up on teachings about "signs following the believer".[1] But I have a problem with miracles. My problem is that although I believe in them, I can't believe how seldom I see them. And it's only made worse by the fact that those parts of the Christian world which claim God is a God of miracles seem to have barely any more evidence to show for their belief than those who say that miracles vanished with the death of the apostles.[2]

The notion that God can move in our physical world, responding in miraculous ways, has been a longstanding topic of debate for Christians.[3] Spiritual phenomena, gifts of the Spirit, and miracles all took centre stage in some of the old battles between the historic churches and the emerging Pentecostal movements in the early twentieth century.

The debate was given a fresh surge of energy with the charismatic movement of the 1960s to 1980s. Pentecostals thought their clothes had been stolen by the new and more middle-class encounter with the Holy Spirit. The new emphasis on the restoration of the church as the radical presence of the kingdom together with apostolic leadership radicalized the priesthood of all believers. Now everyone was told they had a spiritual gift, and a polite curtain was drawn between the old Pentecostal order and the new house church phenomena. Like a car with a souped-up engine, the charismatic movement appeared to outrun Pentecostalism in its own lane. But in true Protestant spirit, it wasn't long before new fractures appeared.[4]

But these waves of reviving and refreshing which had the biggest impact on Christian faith also widened the chasms of division within evangelical unity. Non-charismatics (for want of a better word) did not take kindly to evangelical spiritualities which embraced miraculous phenomena. In fact, until the 1950s relationships between Pentecostals and the Evangelical Alliance were very difficult. And even though greater levels of tolerance developed between charismatics and non-charismatics in later years, the two remain uncomfortable bed-fellows.

Then came the 1990s and the "Toronto Blessing", which stretched the uneasy accommodation between the two biblical worldviews to a quiet breaking point. On the whole the charismatics and Pentecostals were accommodating. But the more conservative evangelicals were ill at ease, with some even denouncing it as delusional or demonic.

I saw this painfully demonstrated during a consultation in Northern Ireland which was attempting to create greater theological understanding on both sides of the debate. During the opening prayer there was a scraping of the floor, footsteps and the creaking of the door. When we finished the debate and closed in prayer, the noises happened again. I learned afterwards that the man who had left during the prayers did so because he was quite convinced that praying with people sympathetic to Toronto was compromising with demonic spirits!

When the Evangelical Alliance UK hosted a twenty-four-hour consultation for twenty-four leaders on the Toronto phenomena in 1994, our statement was deeply pastoral but not particularly cutting-edge.[5] In truth I felt that a slow and silent drifting apart of theological positions had in fact accelerated.

This silent drift wasn't just to do with how we understood the Holy Spirit or what the Bible had to say about behaviour in worship. Frankly, the animal noises, exuberance and shear physicality of many meetings were difficult to proof-text from the Bible! The problem was also to do with how we were perceived by a rational and cynical world looking for chances to ridicule and caricature the church. Toronto was a perfect gift for cynics on the lookout for a good anti-church story.

So we have all arrived in the twenty-first century to discover that our attitudes towards the Bible, spiritual gifts and worship have become a check-list for our contentions with each other. As has the idea of miracles.

Why is it that so many Bible-believing Christians are decidedly uncomfortable about the miraculous? Generally speaking, evangelicals on the theological right and so-called liberal Christians on the left both come to this issue with equal unrest. This is due in part to the fact that their biblical framework is more comfortable with a modern rationalism in which the inexplicable is mistrusted: if we can't explain it, it's not credible. And if it's not intellectually plausible then it stands to damage the credible claims of the gospel. Better to say, as the liberals do, that miracles in the Bible were myths and never really happened, or to say, as the ultra-conservative evangelicals might do, that they stopped abruptly with the death of the apostles and the emergence of the canon of scripture. Anything more is not to be believed. When it comes to healing, the most adventurous prayer here is likely to sound something like: "If it be thy will that ..."

> The problem was how we were perceived by a rational and cynical world looking for chances to ridicule and caricature the church.

Any talk of healing in this setting is a theological nuisance because it smacks of bossing God around to do something he has lost interest in doing. In any event, God's sovereignty means he heals if and when he wants to. Consequently, there's not much point in making too much of a fuss about it. A brief formal prayer will do: nothing dramatic should be expected. Generally, conservatives don't like miracles and the inexplicable because if you believe in them you are in danger of losing intellectual control.

This attitude towards miracles and healing is often further strengthened by the drama so often associated with them. Huge statements about "your miracle" which have come to typify televangelist culture can be an embarrassment to thinking people. Big claims with small accountability seriously undermine credibility. Big claims which link miracles and healings to financial contributions are really bad news for the good news. And the bitter reality of the multitudes who walk away from the prayer line without healing or pastoral support is a discredit to the Christ who never made a promise of healing he didn't deliver.

> Generally, conservatives don't like miracles and the inexplicable because if you believe in them you are in danger of losing intellectual control.

Healing ministries are not always entirely honest: they seldom tell us about the sick ones "who got away". They don't always say, "Not everyone gets healed every time." They fail to point out that Elisha the prophet died of a terminal illness, not old age.[6]

They never wrestle with the mystery of miracle healers such as Smith Wigglesworth who died of a stroke in his eighties; Stephen Jeffries, "the healing evangelist", whose health began to fail in his mid-thirties and who died crippled with arthritis at fifty-nine[7] or David Watson and John Wimber whose deaths rocked the charismatic world.

The growing post-evangelical, post-charismatic community is populated by a quiet continent of disillusioned people who have lived through failed promises and who cannot work out whether to blame God, themselves or the pastor-apostle. These people sit at home and shake their heads in disbelief: for they went to Pensacola and Toronto Vineyard and have no answers to explain the empty shells of movements in which they once believed.

Miracles, then, are a problem. Christianity is more logical and predictable without them. The mysterious is, quite frankly, messy.

But that is precisely the point: mysteries by definition are indefinable. And much as it may confuse us, God likes that. For our rational arguements are only a part of what makes the Bible believable. Ultimately the credibility of the Bible is in fact its incredulity.[8] What makes Christ credible is not our ability to describe him coherently with the words we use about him. It is his own ability to captivate our minds by his inexplicable wonders. What made Christ credible in the upper room explosion had as much to do with miracles[9] as it had to do with Peter's clear explanation about them.[10]

In January 2006, Lord Hastings was invited to address a conference of evangelical leaders to talk about a Christian strategy for transformation.[11] What he brought instead was a piercing question. What, he asked, is the thing people in our world most long for? His answer, quite simply, is happiness. And what, he wondered, is the route to a recovery of happiness, hope or Shalom? It is, he said, the rumour of angels: an awareness that God is supernaturally at work in our world.

Miracles may come with a lot of baggage but we still need them on the journey. Evangelical Christians believe that the

> Our rational arguements are only a part of what makes the Bible believable. Ultimately the credibility of the Bible is in fact its incredulity.

miracles of the Old and New Testaments are historically reliable. But any casual study of the Christian church, from the early Fathers through to the Montanists, Celtic Christians and the revivals under the Wesleys or Jonathan Edwards, will recognise that there was an inseparable link between the proclamation of good news and the inexplicable wonders of God.

This is precisely why God has stirred great prayer movements across the world in the past two decades. Prayer is on the agenda because it has always been the prelude to God's transforming work in our world.

When Dr Leslie Griffiths, minister at Wesley's Chapel in London, gave me a guided tour of Wesley's house some years ago, our final stop was a small and uneventful room tucked away in the building. "This is where Methodism happened," said Leslie, "it's Wesley's prayer room!" It was a very special moment.

Anyone who has seen the Transformation[12] videos, trailed the growth of the Global Day of Prayer, or participated in 24/7 will know of the numerous stories of personal transformation and communities which have been touched by God's response to our prayers.

No Christian movement has ever changed anything without prayer because prayer is a prelude to miracles.

In *The Conversion of Europe,* Richard Fletcher makes the point quite powerfully. His book provides a study of how it was that the Christian faith fanned its way across pagan Europe between 371 to 1386 AD when it had no biblical language with which to communicate the Christian gospel. According to Fletcher, "Miracles, wonders, exorcisms, temple-torching and shrine-smashing *were in themselves* acts of evangelization."[13] This is not to

No Christian movement has ever changed anything without prayer because prayer is a prelude to miracles.

commend this as a contemporary strategy for evangelism! But the point is well made.

Christians who empty the gospel of the miraculous are dumbing down its truth. It is one thing to say that in the pampered communities of the affluent west reliance on the miraculous has become an optional extra, but it is quite another thing to reject miracles completely because we see so little of them. It's like saying that endangered species do not exist because we do not see them in our local zoo. And it is one thing to shield ourselves from the miraculous because we have been hurt by our own disappointments and quite another to dismiss them as a liability to credible faith.

The plain truth is that Christians who deny the place of miracles may wake up to find that we are out of step with a contemporary culture growing weary with "reason", which changes nothing and no one. In today's world we are emerging from the intellectual confines of modernity into an open space where the weird and wonderful have become normal.

The church is unlikely to present Christ credibly by denying miracles. It may be worth asking whether there is a direct correlation between the universal growth of Pentecostalism[14] and its bold – if perhaps overstated – claims about miracles. Or between the precarious survivalism of older movements and their discomfort with the very idea of the miraculous. It seems quite clear that where the church is growing globally, it is generally less anxious about using the word "miracle".

Christians who empty the gospel of the miraculous are dumbing down its truth. Christians who deny the place of miracles may wake up to find that we are out of step with a contemporary culture growing weary with "reason", which changes nothing and no one.

CHRIST THE CONVERSATIONALIST

I was only half awake as I waited in Entebbe Airport for an early Sunday morning flight. Not far from where I was sitting a group of Londoners heading home engaged in deep conversation. I paid little attention until, through the fog of my tiredness, I overheard that they were talking about "born-again" Christians.

"Yeah, it's the ones who do that thing of talking to you in a low voice you've got to watch. 'Cause, you know, you really have to lean in and it forces you to listen," a man said. "I know," a woman with a squeaky voice joined in. "One of 'em used to get on my train, and he used to ask you lots of questions. And before you knew it, you'd be nodding your head and everything! But I worked *him* out in the end!" she triumphed.

Obviously the "born-againers" didn't make any converts, but evidently their enquiring approach had left some kind of an impression.

It's good to ask questions. There's something irritating about people who talk at you for hours without ever asking anything in return. They're usually quite nice and well-intentioned, but their blind spot is simply that they are self-possessed, filled with the immediacy of their own experiences, pain, adventures or plans. So much so that they fail to pause long enough to step into another person's reality. Sometimes they're simply so filled with the rightness of their own position that they are incapable of accommodating another point of view.

Mostly these people mean well. But they don't make the best company.

Some non-listeners are just too insecure to ask a question. The truth is that it takes a certain confidence to do so because questions are like walkways into other people's hearts or crow-bars into safety vaults. If you open things up then you need to be able to handle what you find.

It's always a lot easier to just talk and hope that you are being heard.

But it's not easy to stop talking when you passionately believe that what you have to say really will do other people a lot of good. It's as hard as imagining Alexander Fleming having just discovered penicillin and then sitting quietly in his room to do the crossword. People who believe that the gospel is good news have a certain compulsion to talk it up. And that compulsion is even greater when there has been a great commission to do so. For people who have come into a living, loving relationship with God, it's a moral offence to be silent. If your life has *truly* been changed you will really want others to know about it.

And if you truly walk in the Truth then it's hard to ignore a half-truth when one's coming towards you.

Evangelicals are passionate about biblical truth. And in an age when truth has rapidly become personalised and margina-lised, evangelicals, more than many other brands of Christian, are apt to rush to its defence. And rightly so. If there is such a thing as revealed truth, then to ignore it is not only an affront to God, it's also bad for our health. When society marginalises a biblical view on marriage or sexuality and we see excessive divorce rates and unprecedented levels of teenage pregnancy and sexually transmitted disease, we want to talk about it. There's something about society's malfunction which drives us to fire off urgent press statements rather than sit down for ponderous, discursive press conferences.

Evangelicals not only helped to shape modernity, they have also been greatly influenced by it. We are therefore more comfortable with propositional warfare about truth from a distance than we are with discourse at close range. The word "dialogue" has only been cautiously received in the evangelical lexicon in the last decade. Evangelicals hate doctrinal fog with a passion and deplore driving in the moral twilight zone. What we have to offer is "assurance of faith", not debates about doubting.

> There's something about society's malfunction which drives us to fire off urgent press statements rather than sit down for ponderous, discursive press conferences.

But the problem is that beneath all this assurance we're also afraid. And people who are afraid tend to talk a lot. We're afraid of losing truth as we understand it. Often this is not in fact the truth of biblical authority, but the "truth" decided by evangelical sub-cultures which try to claim the right to define what is acceptable and what is not. But it's worth remembering that perfect love rejects all types of fear, including our fear that we will lose our grip on truth.[1] The fact of the matter is that for too many evangelicals, holiness is synonymous with a sense of anxiety about the world and our relationship to it.[2]

And we are also afraid of our sacred spaces now being occupied by other faiths. We are concerned that our reserved seats at the places of influence have been taken away. We are losing our "Christian heritage". We have noted the growth and influence of Islam. We feel powerless about the secular onslaught in the press and media which positions Christianity as an embarrassing imperial power to be beaten down and discarded.

And so we respond by shouting, convinced we must do so in order to be heard.

Unfortunately, people are unlikely to listen to what you have to say if you start off by shouting at them. Twenty-first century evangelicals should take a leaf out of Jesus' book: conversations are so much better. Our earliest example of Jesus' ministry was his dazzling display of wisdom – at the age of twelve. The easiest thing is to suppose that Jesus was lecturing the grown ups; in fact he was as busy listening and asking as he was answering questions.[3] Jesus did not rush around Palestine pontificating from great heights. Yes, he spoke authoritatively and left the opposition standing, but in true rabbinic style he also raised questions and innuendoes which helped people find the answers to their own needs.

Jesus was a consummate conversationalist. His life-changing questions and discourses would often precede great personal healings. Even on the cross he had time for a conversation with thieves. And finally he left the planet having raised a massive question.[4]

Questions and curiosity are the hallmarks of a confident church. People who are confident give themselves permission not to know some things because they are certain of what they *do* know. The idea that we never ask for other people's opinions (no questions please, we're Christians!) is a betrayal of New Testament engagement. Neither Paul nor Peter would be comfortable with it. It's worth remembering that two of the most austere Old Testament books end with questions.[5] Questions make us informed "healers" because they invite reflective self-assessment in those with whom we dialogue. There can't be too many people who would happily swallow tablets prescribed by a doctor who neither looked at them nor asked questions about their pain!

The challenge of our day is to get involved in the conversations of our times in order to bring godly perspectives to the debate.[6] We should never assume that no one wants to hear a whisper from the church. People "out there" still want to hear what Christians think about a host of contemporary issues, not least because our political leaders seem to have very few solutions. This was precisely the enduring strength of eighteenth- and nineteenth-century evangelicalism in Britain and the US which became totally implicated in the spiritual, social, economic and political life of the nation.

Credible Christian faith must not cower from public discourse. Rob Bell is right to remind us that "the world around us shifts, and the Christian faith is alive only when it is listening, morphing, innovating, letting go of whatever has gotten in the way of Jesus".[7]

> The challenge of our day is to get involved in the conversations of our times in order to bring godly perspectives to the debate.

I had an exhilarating afternoon conversation with Luis Palau[8] in which he told me of his "Riverside Talks" with a senior Chinese politician. The book of the talks – billed as "A friendly dialogue between an atheist and a Christian" – became a best-seller across China.

In a culture confused by the loss of values, what do evangelicals have to offer? If people are talking about critical issues such as trust, hope and respect, what better openings could there be for a biblical perspective?[9] In South Africa, the Heartlines project has used precisely these sorts of openings, creating professionally produced life dramas on current social and moral issues. The unashamedly Christian perspectives on critical areas such as AIDS/HIV, drugs, faithfulness and reconciliation have gained widespread acceptance on major TV channels there. There are now similar plans to televise them across other African countries.

When we lack the confidence or energy to ask intelligent questions of our culture, our default position is to hurl advice from the safety of our pulpits and insular conferences. We end up head-butting our world in the name of love.

But warfare with our culture is not very productive[10] or even typical of the New Testament. The early church spent a lot of time opposing sin, but it was also very good at *colonising* the culture for Christ. What we now know as Christmas, Easter, and Sunday worship were formerly pagan. The church even hijacked the language of its time: "logos", "gospel", "redemption" and "church" were all colonised. The New Testament is a lexicon of borrowed words and ideas.

In championing the truth that we are so passionate about, evangelicals often seem to be proud of a contentiousness which marks us out from other people. But is this biblical? It's not that we set out to be ungracious; maybe we are just more fearful and lethargic about truth than we care to admit. When one thinks how hard it must have been to colonise Greek words and Roman habits, then perhaps we can appreciate how much harder we need to work at engaging our own culture with our truth.

Preaching, teaching and witnessing need to become less complacent. We must stop telling others what we think they *want to* hear rather than what they actually need to know. And we must think increasingly about the way in which our listeners hear. Modern society's chat-show culture is more open to a church unafraid to sit around an Alpha supper table and talk about the meaning of life. It will engage with pointed discussions about Mark's gospel and its view of sin and repentance as presented by groups such as Christianity Explored. It will consider evangelist J.John's upbeat and contemporary presentation of the Ten Commandments, which relate them to everyday relationships. When we enter into dialogue, sinners are given the dignity of choice and the option not to be fully persuaded.[11]

Undoubtedly, conversational Christianity is more demanding for the local church because it means more than just preaching and worshipping differently; it means *thinking* differently about *who* we are and what we *do* as a result.

Only a conversational church can really be a witnessing church because it can never fully understand itself unless it is in conversation with its world.

Conversational evangelicalism is unlikely to emerge from a siege mentality which sets itself against the culture. It can only spring from churches dedicated to producing confident subversives. These will be individuals who know themselves well enough to get involved in the conversations without losing their message. Only as we morph into "learning communities"[12] are we more likely to become the kind of biblical evangelicals who reflect New Testament vitality.

> Conversational Christianity is more demanding because it means more than just preaching and worshipping differently; it means *thinking* differently about *who* we are and what we *do* as a result.

Conversational Christianity will present Christ credibly not because it has all of the answers for all of the questions all of the time, but simply because it reflects the spirit of the great conversationalist himself.

5

ROCK STEADY

Someone once said that the church is a little like Noah's ark: it may be a bit smelly on the inside, but at least it's an awful lot safer than what's going on outside!

It's a good metaphor. The popular view of the western church is of an ageing and weather-beaten vessel, reeking with irrelevance and rocked by controversy. The church struggles with secular culture and with the rapid images and values of its environment. Churches are seen as "anti" everything, low on tolerance and high on arrogance. And evangelicals are, of course, the worst of the bunch – the new fundamentalists. For every ten positive stories about the church, it seems, another ten appear to drown out the good news.

The internal realities only add to the problem. Our church buildings contain thousands of faithful worshippers singing about experiences they no longer have in the same choruses they sang the week before, listening to sermons which make them laugh without building them up. Even in places with phenomenal church growth, like Africa, the church is described as a mile wide and an inch deep. Generally speaking we have a lot more Christians than we do disciples.

Like the ark, the church sometimes stinks. But in a strange way, it is still stubbornly glorious! And, despite its pungency, every single Christian leader I spoke to in the process of writing this book implicated the church in the job of "presenting Christ credibly to society".

In this vital task, the bewildering truth is that God has appointed his church as the sole PR agent for the reputation of his son.

Christ is credible. In the marketplace of choices he may not be comfortable or convenient, but he is believable and viable: Christ as a real man dealing with real issues in a real world. Our mission is not to *make* him credible but to *unveil* him as such. As Pilate said, "Here is the man!"[1] But, as everybody knows, credible people still get rejected. Credibility is no guarantee of acceptance. But it helps.

> Our mission is not to *make* Christ credible but to *unveil* him as such.

The main task of the church then is not to fight its corner in the public square. Nor is it to scream for its rights or snatch back lost privileges. It is certainly not to gain credit points from the culture. Instead it is, as Archbishop of York John Sentamu reminded the audience at his inaugural service, to present Christ as a credible option for people looking for God.[2]

It's a universal issue. In Dublin, politics and materialism are rapidly undermining Christian credibility. In places like Peru, Ecuador, Paraguay and Bolivia, Jesus often needs to be re-presented to Christianised people as someone other than the victorious Portuguese Christ who conquered the Latino.[3] Today many African-Americans are still hostile towards a European Jesus who made Africans slaves.

Central to the credibility mission is the issue of biblicism in the life of the church. We have access to more than five hundred versions of the Bible in over two thousand languages. Yet, even with such a surfeit of biblical resources, study guides and electronic Bible gadgets, biblical awareness is plummeting. Christians can spend decades in churches without a credible view of the biblical Jesus.

We simply must *biblicise the church*. This does not mean more Bible study notes for western churches that already have enough. Nor does it mean more Christian organisations. In fact, one of the greatest gifts to the body of Christ today might actually be a streamlining of existing resources and organisations to respond to this challenge.

Neither is this an attempt to get Christians to proof-text the Bible in their preaching. Beyond the task of getting evangelicals to dutifully plough through the scriptures, biblicising the church is about inspiring a love for the Bible, discovering its purpose and power to work within the uncertainties of our contemporary culture, and enabling evangelicals to engage people with the story through conversation. Rob Bell puts it really well: "We have to embrace the Bible as the wild, uncensored, passionate account it is of people experiencing the living God."[4]

Biblicising the church means to get Christians to love the scriptures in order to study the Bible. Because only a biblicised church has the energy and courage to strip away the barriers between us and Jesus. In my conversations with Bishop Tom Wright, he stressed that we need to re-discover the Christ of the gospels – not just the systematic letters of Paul.[5]

Secondly, we need a church which behaves intelligently.

An intelligent church is a *prayed-through* church because it really believes that God moves in response to our relationship with him. No church seriously committed to our world can cease to pray and intercede for it. It is no coincidence that movements such as the Global Day of Prayer and 24/7 have seen such amazing stories of people with changed lives and circumstances. Over the past decade the Transformation prayer movement has also reported significant stories of community transformation through prayer. And it's not unusual now to see reports of police operations which work in partnership with local prayer initiatives.

And an intelligent church is also a *thought-through* church. This takes nothing away from the points we raised in chapter three, "Rumours of Angels", supporting the role of miracles and divine interventions. Nothing can take the place of the miraculous, but the Spirit is also always happy to work with rational, intelligent material.

A thought-through church thinks about what it says. If every preacher assumed that in their congregation were people with life experiences superior to their own – a math professor perhaps, or a senior judge, molecular scientist or cabinet minister – then I suspect the preaching would turn out to be far more credible. Sometimes preachers say stupid things simply because they know they can get away with it.

Thirdly, thought-through churches have a credibility challenge in trying to raise the bar on moral conduct, and not only in the area of sexual behaviour. Sexual ethics are important but so too is our conduct in business, our response to the poor and our stewardship of the environment. Today's culture may well come to understand our personal holiness through what they see of our ethical responsibility.[6]

In fact, a courageous and really thought-through approach may well be to *model* morality a lot more and talk about it a lot less – particularly given that some of the old issues have long since become political rather than purely moral issues.

The bald truth is that in popular perception, the evangelical church lost the moral battles thirty years ago and, although there are hopeful signs that society's moral desperation is leading it back to its senses, we may well have another generation before our faithful voices will be properly heard on this agenda.

Luis Palau put it like this: "Homosexuality and abortion are no longer merely moral issues. They have become political issues which evangelicals are being drawn into. Evangelicals are not acting cowardly if we do not speak out constantly on these issues. It's not compromise."[7]

> Thought-through churches have a credibility challenge in trying to raise the bar on moral conduct, and not only in the area of sexual behaviour.

Fourthly, a credible Christ will become known only as a result of what we do in his name. On a flight from Germany to Brazil, Dr Bertil Ekstom sat next to a young woman who showed little interest in his theological views until he mentioned that he was also working with street children in Brazil. As Ekstom says: "What gives credibility is not our doctrines for which I can give ten points. It's the true coherence between our confession of Christ, the love of God and our practical action in society."[8]

As evangelicals we are deluded if we believe that credibility depends entirely on well mapped-out ideas about God. Reason and coherence are vital, but people also want a God who does things. A credible Christ "has to be trusted to meet the needs of the community".[9]

When we get this right, people notice.

After hurricane Katrina swept through New Orleans in the United States in September 2005, former UK Labour Party minister and committed atheist Roy Hattersley made a startling admission in his analysis of the Salvation Army's response to the disaster. He admitted that he could neither accept the contradictions he saw in the Bible nor the claims about miracles. But he was still full of admiration for Christians. Here's how he put it: "The only possible conclusion is that faith comes with a packet of moral imperatives that, while they do not condition the attitude of all believers, influence enough of them to make them morally superior to atheists like me. The truth may make us free but it has not made us as admirable as the average captain in the Salvation Army."[10]

This is the heritage of nineteenth-century evangelicalism, but since the 1930s and the paranoia over the social gospel, some sections of evangelicalism have lost sight of the centrality of social action to our faith. Admittedly for many evangelicals the late 1970s began to see "acts of kindness" becoming part and parcel of evangelical witness once more. This needs to be so for all of us. Whatever the headlines have to say about Christian faith in general and evangelicalism in particular, our credibility rests on social action becoming a hallmark of the Christian faith.

Our credibility rests on social action becoming a hallmark of the Christian faith.

One final point: credibility has a lot to do with confidence. A self-deprecating Saviour is a contradiction. What is needed in evangelical faith is to recover a confidence in ourselves as ambassadors to our culture.

We don't have to be cocky in our confidence. We know our weaknesses only too well for that. Our credible confidence has to do with the incredible power of our mission in the world. And it also has a lot to do with the fact that we are at one with Christ in that mission.

An evangelicalism fit for the twenty-first century will believe Christ's analysis about the church's future rather than that given by the contemporary press. And it will come to realise a stupendous fact: Jesus has locked his credibility into ours, placed the future of his church on our feeble shoulders and commanded us to go to the ends of the world.

PART 2

REHABILITATING "EVANGELICAL" AS GOOD NEWS

> *"He has commissioned me to announce the breaking news – top news for the poor; He's sent me to mend broken hearts, to liberate those slammed up in dark prisons, to announce good – that this is the era of God going gentle on his people."*
>
> —Luke 4:18–19 (The Word on the Street)

"The problem with words," said the late playwright Dennis Potter, "is that you never know where they've been!"

Words are such temperamental and transitory tools. They have no fixed abode. They change their nuances and meanings depending on what certain people in certain places at certain times decide they mean. If you don't believe me just read the Bible. In it you will find words in the Authorised Version we no longer use in polite company!

Good words can go bad and bad words can become respectable. These changes often have a lot to do with things we do to words by the actions we take. But they also have an awful lot to do with what opinion formers and propagandists tell us about the meaning of words.

Nowhere is this more relevant than with the word "evangelical".

If you had the nerve to walk through your local shopping mall with a banner saying "I am an evangelical", the responses you almost certainly would get would be the product of how the word has been shaped both by evangelicals' behaviour as well as by what people say about them. Some of those responses would also come out of sheer ignorance.

But words can change their meaning. Once upon a time a "West Indian" was a "white plantation owner" and "gay" meant "happy". And no one has more power to change what words mean than the people who own those words.

There are over 420 million evangelicals in the world. If they really wanted it to happen, then "evangelical" could mean *good news*.

WHAT'S IN A NAME?

There is something very quaint about the word "evangelical". It feels somehow otherworldly. In many ways it has no ties to the natural world. It's not a denomination and it has no cathedrals. The restless cultures within evangelicalism have ensured it has been impervious to institutional formation.

It's tough to tie it down.

And identifying *an evangelical* is no easier. My son and I have the same first name. When my wife yelled out "Joel!" from any part of the house, both of us knew instinctively which one of us she was calling. It was a domestic marvel. Three years ago he moved out, but when we were together again as a family for a Christmas Day meal, my wife yelled out "Joel" and *both* of us answered. My daughter thinks it was because we weren't all living together anymore. We had lost a familial element.

In the same way, if you call out "evangelical" these days, you never quite know who is going to answer you. Evangelicals now make up a big, extended family in which legitimate membership has drifted across cultures, church styles, and doctrinal emphases. It has even crossed the Reformation divide into Catholicism. Evangelicals are "open", "progressive",

"mainstream", left and right, "post" or "radical", "conservative" or "fundamental". They can be charismatic, Pentecostal
or Reformed.

They also cross political allegiances. A few years ago I
attended a Baptist church in America with a visiting preacher.
After the meeting we went to a nearby restaurant for an evening
meal. "Is it true that in Britain evangelicals can vote Labour?"
he asked earnestly. I said they could and that evangelicals in
the UK were as politically divided as the rest of the population.
He was amazed. He leaned forward, looked furtively around
and lowered his voice. "In the last election I voted Democrat!"
he said. I pretended I was shocked.

Evangelical identity has always been hard to pin down. In
1996 the first publication of the Evangelical Alliance's new
theological commission was "What is an evangelical?" Actually it's a very old question. Lord Shaftesbury complained
that whilst in former times he knew what an evangelical was,
he later had "no clear notion of what constitutes one now".
Charles Spurgeon had the same problem: "It is a mere cant to
cry, 'We are evangelical, we are evangelical' and yet decline to
say what evangelical means."

The problem of evangelical identity has always been intensified by
the fact that evangelicals love tidy
and systematic categories with which
to work. We would never have coped
with the ambiguities of the emerging
New Testament church.

Unfortunately, the issue of evangelical identity is so often determined by what we are *not* and by
what others are *not* allowed to be. Subtle shades have no place
in our world. Whether you are in or out largely depends on

who is making those decisions. So, in the early years of the twentieth century, Pentecostals were not allowed to be called evangelicals and appeared on the outskirts of Billy Graham's crusades.[1] In the 1960s to 1980s, charismatic Christians were the mistrusted newcomers. Now cultural expressions of church from Asia, Africa and Latin America are reshaping the evangelical family, both enriching and enraging some of the old norms.

Deciding who's in and who's out is quite a job. Here's how we might begin to approach this global task.

- The first thing to recognise is that evangelical identity has always been hard to establish. And it should be hard. It is worked out in the complex mix of biblical truth, personal histories and social action. It has been radical and reforming, retiring and cautious, Eurocentric in the past and now led by the global south.

- No one evangelical subculture has the right to decide what an evangelical is. Evangelical identity should be shaped by cultural blenders which work within the constraints of orthodox faith. It should be biblically solid at the core but culturally flexible on the edges. Evangelicalism is big enough to accommodate someone who embraces a doctrine of material prosperity as well as someone who believes that we are predestined to be saved.

- Evangelicals should never use truth primarily to exclude others. Truth has come to set us free. A kingdom-minded evangelical *begins* a spiritual relationship with a commitment to *include* the other person and only then tests that relationship with what the Bible says.[2] This is a point Brian McLaren is keen to make: "The kingdom of God seeks to include all who want to participate in and contribute to its purpose, but it cannot include those who oppose its purpose."[3]

- When evangelical Christians set themselves up as final arbiters of truth, they are on very dangerous ground. This is the stuff of which spiritual mafias are made. I am very weary of "gospel churches" who alone decide what a "gospel church" is. Usually their definition turns out to be remarkably similar to what they look like.

- Evangelicals should be recognised by a commitment to the Bible and its authority in all matters of doctrine and ethics. But no single cultural interpretation can be allowed to dominate. By an unspoken global agreement of grace, evangelicals are drawn together across many different cultures. What should however be universal are our pietism, moral codes and political radicalism. As a result all evangelicals are wedded to orthodoxy, but we are also aware that orthodoxy will always be bigger than evangelicals. In identifying what it means to be a Christian, evangelicals have a key role to play. But evangelicalism is not orthodoxy. Nor have evangelicals been appointed as God's thought police.

> When evangelical Christians set themselves up as final arbiters of truth, they are on very dangerous ground. This is the stuff of which spiritual mafias are made.

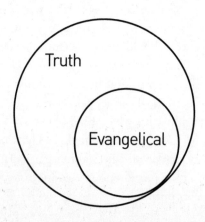

- Evangelicals should deal harshly with people who invoke the doctrine of "guilt by association". This pernicious practice works in the name of truth but in fact betrays it because it usually operates independently of facts. Not too long ago I wrote an article in which I quoted a liberal theologian. In response, a member of the Evangelical Alliance wrote in to complain that I had changed allegiance and was taking the entire Alliance with me! And it was only a short quote!

- Evangelical faith is misrepresented if it is reduced to a narrow moral agenda at the expense of wider ethical issues. Those who stand against abortion and legislation supporting gay rights must also campaign for justice and defend the poor.[4]

- God is not party-political. The fact that American Republicanism is no longer a synonym for evangelicalism is good news for the gospel. God is no more *against* the African National Congress than he is *for* the Republican Right.[5] At a time when global politics is most in need of hope and practical solutions it would be a tragedy for evangelical Christians to scrap over political power and different ways of doing things. Christian politicians in Britain have an excellent model in the G6, six cross-party evangelicals who vote very differently but who share regular fellowship in the context of their political life. Evangelicals must learn to emulate this model. Our greatest mistake as we operate in the public square would be to decide our evangelical status on how we vote on particular issues. Public policy stances do not define our faith. We should be prepared to die together for Jesus – but we should never crucify each other on the basis of our vote.

None of the above is to say that evangelical identity lacks some defining points. Whatever we may make of the word "evangelical", we simply cannot escape its biblical underpinning. From its New Testament "gospel" roots to the Reformation and into the twenty-first century, the *evangel* – good news – is central to evangelical identity.

> Public policy stances do not define our faith. We should be prepared to die together for Jesus – but we should never crucify each other on the basis of our vote.

As far as the World Evangelical Alliance (WEA) is concerned, being evangelical begins with a personal relationship with Christ and living out the gospel. WEA's "Case for Support"[6] briefly compares David Bebbington's definition[7] with John Stott's approach. For Bebbington, evangelical means:

- Biblical authority
- Christ at the centre
- Conversion
- Social action

Stott, who is very keen to avoid the label "evangelicalism", views evangelical faith fundamentally as one which has the doctrine of the Trinity at its heart.[8]

The strength and tenacity of evangelical faith have nothing to do with cultural preferences, which so often lead to prejudices. And they are definitely not to do with brand-pride in "the big E". There is nothing worth dying for in the label. But instead it is evangelicalism's biblical worldview and its tendency to change people and places which carry the day.

Its strength has everything to do with its good news impulse. And that good news urge always takes seriously Jesus as the living Word, reigning at the centre of the universe and our lives. Evangelicals will not swap his lordship for our culture. They are absolutely passionate about renewed people and communities which treat sin and forgiveness seriously.

Evangelicals really do want to see God ruling everything. And they know that none of this is possible without the active and indwelling work of his Spirit.

The twenty-first century will pull us in many different directions, but these are the things we should die for.

A GOOD TIME TO BE GOOD (NEWS)

Humanists have a real problem. After two hundred years of the secular experiment, religion refuses to go away. The old atheist communist block has collapsed, and even China shows signs of going softer on religion. And many of the new political menaces are now dressed in religious garb.

Karl Marx will not be the driving force of African growth. It will either be Mohammed or Jesus. We have presidents and prime ministers who wear their faith on their sleeves, and transparent and deliberate partnerships between governments and faith groups. World news is now unimaginable without stories driven by religion. In a recent conversation, a Christian politician in Britain told me he has never known a time when there were so many Christians in the House of Commons.

Faith has certainly not gone on vacation.

So given all of that, at a time when faith and religion are becoming more fashionable, why are a growing number of evangelicals seeking to abandon the label "evangelical"?

Evangelicals, it seems, are aware that the word is not always understood and is often misrepresented. A number of evangelical movements have in fact re-branded in order to leave the label behind. When the conservative British

Evangelical Council re-launched in 2004, it was under the name "Affinity".

"Evangelical" appears to have a PR problem; we are all afraid of what it means to outsiders.

"Evangelical" appears to have a PR problem; we are all afraid of what it means to outsiders.

Tony Campolo told me that he feels the label "raises red flags" and erects barricades to the gospel. Campolo is working with a small group of people to use the name "Red Letter Christians" as an alternative (the phrase is a reference to the use of red lettering for the words of Christ in some versions of the Bible).[1] And although Stuart Murray-Williams uses "evangelical" as one of his self-descriptions, he admits that he finds it embarrassing. Murray-Williams' dilemma is that he cannot think of a suitable alternative.[2] Surprisingly, perhaps, Peter Jenson, Anglican Archbishop of Sydney, doubts that the word "is easily recoverable for the outside world" and feels it communicates "nothing of value to secular people". Yet, in spite of this he sees it as a "rallying point for Christians of a certain type".[3]

Quite apart from these well-known names there is a growing brood of younger people who feel that "evangelicalism" is either irrelevant or irritating. They are impatient with its conservatism, bored by its worship, and unconvinced by what they think of as a limited moral agenda. They flinch at discussions about human sexuality and wonder why their leaders are not on the demonstrations against injustice.

Having said that, there are pockets of church life where the significant growth is amongst younger conservative evangelicals. Not everything has to do with age.

Evangelicals, then, have a choice: carry out a global competition to find a better name to describe our odd distinctives, or work together to strip away the caricatures we have helped to create and rehabilitate "evangelical" as good news to our world.

Here are my perspectives as to why we should keep the name:

- The word "evangelical" has a biblical root in "evangel", meaning "good news". This gives it theological weight and authenticity.
- It has a powerful and engaging heritage. Like a Russian doll, it opens up to reveal a movement with a track record in radicalism, political reform and social engagement, along with piety, evangelism, preaching, scholarship and transforming prayer. It also has important moral scruples which we lose at society's peril!
- It is identified more than any other word with gospel proclamation and with changed lives. It is associated with the idea of the transformation of the human life.
- It would be a foolish time to drop the name because there are now so many people who identify themselves and are known as evangelicals in strategic places in society. They are advisors, cabinet ministers, broadcasters, partners with local government, environmentalists, social activists and leaders of respected NGOs in the fight against injustice. Evangelicals have been central to global movements such as Jubilee 2000 and Make Poverty History, campaigns they are continuing with Micah Challenge (which is now actively at work in thirty-four nations and recognised by the United Nations and Global Call to Action Against Poverty).
- Evangelicals represent a key growth area in global Christianity. Some time ago the Christian Research Association's Peter Brierley told me there are two growing religious streams in the world: Islam and evangelicalism. In 2004 the *Los Angeles Daily News* claimed that nearly

20 percent of Hispanics had become evangelical. The Association of Evangelicals in Africa (AEA) claims to represent 80–120 million people,[4] and the World Evangelical Alliance represents some 420 million Christians in 128 countries. This means evangelicals make up 6.5 percent of the world's population.[5]

- In my twenty years in evangelical circles, it's been very evident that the wider Christian family has come to appreciate and even embrace evangelicals more than ever before. It's hard to ignore our growth and development. In Britain a third of the House of Bishops and a third of churchgoers across all denominations are evangelical. A 2005 survey in the US revealed that 93 of the top 100 growing churches are evangelical.[6] And according to George Barna's 2006 report, 38 percent of Americans – some 84 million people – describe themselves as "evangelical".[7] There are now few ecumenical movements across the world that do not have or actively seek relationships with evangelical churches.

- Evangelical scholarship has grown beyond its Cinderella status of the 1930s and 1950s to produce some of the world's leading scholars and academic institutions.[8] Stephen Holmes from St Andrew's University describes evangelical academia as "strident and intellectually robust ... being found credible by those who are thinking about it most deeply".[9]

- Evangelicals are passionate about the Bible. We are more inclined to read it literally, and whilst literalism can lead to biblical naivety, on the whole it means that evangelicals retain a healthy respect for its authority, power and relevance to personal life. If Christian faith loses this, all is lost.

- We talk a lot about the lordship of Jesus and seek to put him at the centre of everything. A non-historical Christ of faith is incompatible with evangelical Christian belief. His virgin birth, his life, teaching, death and resurrection are all inseparable from evangelical worship.

- Generally evangelicals are quite creative! The entrepreneurial spirit which drove them into missions, abolitionism and business in the eighteenth and nineteenth centuries is alive and well. They are behind some of the world's most enterprising missions and global and national events. Almost without exception, the world's best known preachers who have come to international prominence have been evangelical. Rightly or wrongly they love and target the media because they think they have a story to tell.

These points are vitally important. It is possible that evangelicals are more bothered by the label than people who are not Christians. There is a real danger that when we recoil from the word, we do so in part as a result of the difficulties which non-evangelical Christians have with us. Having spent a great deal of my ministry in ecumenical settings as well as "secular" meetings, I am aware that "liberal" Christians still find us very awkward and disagreeable on issues such as women's leadership and homosexuality.

A non-historical Christ of faith is incompatible with evangelical Christian belief. His virgin birth, his life, teaching, death and resurrection are all inseparable from evangelical worship.

But there are real indications that, apart from some sections of the secular press who cannot tell the difference between "evangelical" and "tele-evangelist", most people are indifferent towards the term.

If George Barna found 22 percent of Americans favourable towards evangelicals and 23 percent unfavourable, that leaves 55 percent who are open to be persuaded.[10] In 2005 Tearfund

UK carried out two substantial surveys which also showed that 52 percent of people were neutral, 19 percent were positive and 17 percent didn't know. Only 12 percent were negative towards evangelicals.

It's probably helpful to realise that we are a lot more aware of our own embarrassing inadequacies than others are. If you are obsessed with the spot on your nose, you'll probably think everyone else on the bus will go home to tell their family about it!

And this is vital too: no one is able to come up with another label which better describes the theological, moral and transformational distinctive of evangelical Christianity. I have not spoken to anybody who thinks that Campolo's Red Letter Christian idea has legs.[11] Tom Wright said: "'Evangelical' is one of the greatest words in the world!" And Alistair McGrath, who spends a great deal of his working ministry in America, said: "I can't think of a better word to use." Geoff Tunnicliffe, International Director of WEA, said that in his international travels he has yet to discover anyone using a viable alternative.[12]

In Zambia Pentecostal Christians prefer evangelical to charismatic.[13] And given that *evangelho* in Portuguese and *evangelico* in Spanish translates as "gospel", over 80 million Latin Americans have "no escape from the word".[14]

Because there's a lot in a word, there is a lot to lose. And evangelicals – more than anyone else – are responsible for shaping what "evangelical" comes to mean in the twenty-first century.

TO THE LEFT

Evangelical categories are difficult. Who belongs precisely where is a very hard thing to agree on.

But just to make sense of this conversation, let's assume that by "left" I am referring to evangelicals who firmly believe in the central ideas about the Bible as God's inspired word to humankind; that Jesus is the final revelation of God; and that the congenital sin which separates us from him can only be dealt with by the atoning death of Jesus Christ. With some notable exceptions such people are unlikely to be theologically Reformed.

They may or may not be charismatic and are as likely to be open to the influence of other, more contemplative spiritualities which do not deny the atoning work of Christ. They are sympathetic to charismatic gifts.

Generally they hold to Christian ethics but are embarrassed by what they see as an overemphasis on sexuality and abortion. They are more committed to social engagement and political activism on issues of global poverty or injustice. They despise prosperity preaching.

People on the left struggle with prescriptive forms of gathered church structure and may find themselves more comfortable in fresh or emerging expressions of church. They may even be monastic (given to a more introverted and liturgical spirituality). The language of ecumenism is irrelevant, and they are comfortable in multi-faith settings. They can be proudly inclusive and tend to be sensitive to culture and how evangelicals come across to the world. They have no problems with women bishops or pastors and won't chide you if you miss the Sunday service to go to the cinema instead!

And they are really impatient with the people who they say give "evangelical" a bad name by their protests, ungracious attitudes and stodgy doctrines (they usually mean evangelicals on the right). They have varying degrees of relationship with evangelicals in the centre.

They're unlikely to be over fifty, but they are not limited to the twenty- to thirty-something bracket either; invariably they hold the evangelical label very lightly.

Everyone reading this will know someone who claims to be left but for whom these categories do not apply! I did say it was difficult.

The evangelical left is nervous about the word "evangelical". They tend to associate it with an over-fifties spiritual club: grey men in black suits who take forever to decide things about which nobody cares. Even though they like many of the moderates they know personally, in their minds evangelicals are yesterday's Christians. They cannot think of another label, but quite frankly they don't see the need for one: "Christian" will do. "Follower of Jesus" is even better.

Secondly, they don't like the word "evangelical" because they have sometimes tended to judge it by its caricatures. They may be unaware of evangelicalism's radical and reforming history: a history of

The evangelical left is nervous about the word "evangelical". They tend to associate it with an over-fifties spiritual club: grey men in black suits who take forever to decide things about which nobody cares.

advocacy for the poor, children, and slaves; education for the young; improvement of working conditions; and the shaping of democracy in Britain and America.[1] They may not know, for example, that the British Labour Party can trace its foundations to evangelical influences and that for a short while after his conversion Keir Hardie – founder of the party – was a member of the Evangelical Union following his conversion under American evangelist Dwight Moody.[2]

Thirdly, people on the left are prone to distance themselves from the word "evangelical" simply because they cannot cope with evangelical fundamentalism. Frankly they are nervous about discussions about homosexuality in the Anglican Communion. They are not necessarily in touch with the theological debate, but they have gay and lesbian friends and just find the whole thing too embarrassing. They hate what seems to be unhelpful and aggressive evangelical homophobia in Australia, Nigeria and Britain. They disagree when evangelicals protest against legislation which tries to deliver equality for everyone. They absolutely want nothing to do with anyone who is fundamentalistic!

And they are really impatient with Christians who talk about sex but have nothing to say about justice. They think it's hypocritical.

Fourthly, people on the left may have a low stigma threshold. It is as though any form of Christianity which puts Christians at odds with the culture is defective. And since evangelical Christianity so often does seem to be at odds with the twenty-first century, there must be something very odd about it. Which is really very odd. The truth of the matter is that a stigma-free church is likely to be in real trouble with God. As the saying

> A stigma-free church is likely to be in real trouble with God. As the saying goes, "He who marries today's culture is likely to be a widower tomorrow."

goes, "He who marries today's culture is likely to be a widower tomorrow."

Squeamish Christians need to remember that throughout its history, the church has often been at its best when its energy and devotion were concentrated by hardship.

My generalisations are of course very dangerous and liable to get me into trouble. Let me lessen the retribution by acknowledging that within the left is a very specific group of people worth highlighting. These are the growing number of evangelical scholars whose reflections increasingly challenge traditional ideas on a range of issues, from our understanding of the atonement to the nature of church. These people have not moved left by default; it has been a considered and progressive migration. Many of them are driven by a genuine passion to engage the church with today's cultural realities.

Where serious theological debate is sparked, it is about how we do missions – not just how we do theology. And that's not entirely a bad thing for evangelicals.

Global evangelicalism needs the people on the left. And it is precisely the issues they feel so strongly about which must be engaged in order to rehabilitate "evangelical" as good news.

Global evangelicalism needs the people on the left.

So here's what we must say to the left:

- If you worship and minister within an evangelical orbit, "evangelical" is still likely to be the best label to describe what you are about. "Christian" is too general to make sense to anyone. In any case, you do need to remember that "Christian" started out as a abusive name.[3] "A follower of Christ" sounds convincing, but I have heard of Hindus who would be happy with that.

- Ironically, people on the left who want to dump the label are in a very good place to help recover the evangelicals' radical heritage. Radicalism, reform, political activism and justice are all a part of its rich history which went missing when evangelicals abandoned social transformation in the 1930s.

- It is undoubtedly hard being associated with extreme evangelicals who sound like fundamentalists. I found evangelicals in Australia and the US reluctant to use the label because they felt it had been hijacked by what they regarded as the fundamentalism of their evangelical neighbors or the Moral Majority agenda of the Christian Coalition in the US. It's certainly good to challenge extremism when it appears, but it's no reason to dump the label. Some people think Jamaicans are all about crime and "bling", but I'm still proud to call myself a Jamaican.

- People on the left need the people in the centre and the people on the right. They shouldn't rubbish the scholarship and diligence of the right with its emphasis on exposition, preaching and scripture. They should buy their books and be willing to sit at their feet. Story-telling is not a substitute for an open Bible on a Sunday morning! Churches without opened Bibles are in danger of becoming closed buildings in the future.

> Story-telling is not a substitute for an open Bible on a Sunday morning! Churches without opened Bibles are in danger of becoming closed buildings in the future.

- But we do need the theological agitation of scholars on the left. The church has to think in fresh ways about its structures, witness and mission. Evangelical complacency needs to be shaken up. Martyn Lloyd-Jones' definition of an evangelical included "the principle of discontinuity".[4]

Having said that, all evangelicals need to recognise that they belong to history and to everybody else. This is one way of ensuring that we avoid the new religion of existential novelty. If you entirely reject the past and its wisdom, you may be in danger of supposing that the church started yesterday and that you are the new St Peter. That is very dangerous for all of us.

History still gives us the best view of the future.

TO THE RIGHT

Evangelical categories are difficult. Who belongs precisely where is a very hard thing to agree on.

But just to make sense of this conversation, let's assume that by "right" I am referring to evangelicals who firmly believe in the central ideas about the Bible as God's inspired word to humankind; that Jesus is the final revelation of God; and that the congenital sin which separates us from him can only be dealt with by the atoning death of Jesus Christ. Such people are likely to be theologically Reformed, dispensational or Arminian.

They are not usually charismatic or open to the influence of other, more contemplative spiritualities – even where these do not deny the atoning work of Christ.

They are not necessarily open to charismatic gifts and differ in their responses to prosperity preaching.

Generally they hold to historic Christian ethics and have a strident opposition to homosexuality and abortion which they will openly condemn as sinful. They support family values. They are cautious about social and political activism on issues of global poverty or injustice, and anxious about a "social gospel" which substitutes social action for gospel proclamation.

People on the right are more comfortable with prescriptive forms of gathered church structure and generally less comfortable with fresh or emerging expressions of church. They will not be monastic. They resist ecumenism as theological compromise and are uncomfortable in multi-faith settings. People on the right are also restless with those who appear in ecumenical or multi-faith settings. They can be proudly exclusive. Some have a keen interest in critiquing culture and are prepared to be scandalised in the world for their faith. Generally they oppose or are uncomfortable with women bishops or pastors and would be disapproving if you missed the Sunday service to go to the cinema instead!

And they are resigned to the risk of giving evangelical a bad name by their uncompromising protests, values and doctrines. They have a very high view of expository or inspirational preaching.

They're likely to be over fifty but there are plenty of thirty-somethings too. Invariably they guard the evangelical label very closely and will sometimes complain that it has been corrupted by those on the left with whom they have little doctrinal patience. They have varying degrees of connectedness with evangelicals in the centre. Usually this depends upon how close specific centre people have gotten to those on the left.

I already know people who claim to be right and for whom these categories do not apply! I did say it was difficult.

Evangelicalism owes a great deal to those on the right. In its formative stages these people were central to the antecedence of evangelicalism. In the fierce intellectual battles against secularisation and liberal faith in the eighteenth and nineteenth centuries, they defended the orthodox positions which gave rise to modern evangelicalism. They were marginalised and ridiculed by their theological rivals. Today's evangelical right in the Anglican Communion and the Baptist movement, for example, have fought gruelling intellectual contests on a range of issues from biblical authority to human sexuality. If you are looking for an evangelical defence of our faith on these matters, you are unlikely to improve on the work done by the right.

Along with this scholarship, those on the right have also contributed incredible preaching and teaching gifts to the body of Christ. As children of modernity they love rationality. In addition, the privileged positions from which many of them have come have helped shape the nature of their input to evangelical faith.

As the old guard of evangelicalism, they were the custodians of the "evangelical" label before Pentecostals and charismatics arrived on the scene. But for the past three decades a massive change has been taking place: the evangelical community has been growing more rapidly amongst Pentecostals and charismatics in the global south, and generally they too want the right to be called evangelical.

Pressed by Christians from different cultural, spiritual and theological perspectives, evangelicals on the right no longer hold the company seal of approval of legitimate evangelical faith, which is why they tend to raise the question "who is an evangelical?" rather more than others.

In broad terms the right is conservative in three areas: theology, morality and politics. In this regard they

Pressed by Christians from different cultural, spiritual and theological perspectives, evangelicals on the right no longer hold the company seal of approval of legitimate evangelical faith, which is why they tend to raise the question "who is an evangelical?" rather more than others.

are likely to draw support from the centre from time to time depending on the issue. But they will seldom ever join forces with the left.

Theologically, people on the right relate to ideas about the Christian faith from the perspective of the sixteenth century, ideas which found new impetus in the theological battles of the twentieth century. Huge theological questions about Jesus, the Bible, salvation and the church are judged against the rubric of the Reformation. In many ways this is an enormous benefit to evangelical faith. The right offers us a constant reminder of where we came from and who we are at the core of our theological being.[1]

But their outlook doesn't necessarily describe where God is taking us and who we have now become in his mission in the world. None of the Reformers or evangelical thinkers of the nineteenth century can help us understand what God did with the incredible growth of the Pentecostal or charismatic movements. For that, we need a lot of the people in the centre and even a few on the left.

Theological superiority which works on the premise that "we were here before you" is not helpful. It's no better than a Roman Catholic saying theirs is the only true church because they knew St Peter before the rest of us.

Be sure that "the scandal we present is the scandal of the cross rather than the scandal of our subcultures."

And if the word "evangelical" is to be good news, then those on the right have an important additional responsibility. As Tom Wright suggested, it is to be sure that "the scandal we present is the scandal of the cross rather than the scandal of our subcultures."[2]

The conservative morality of the evangelical right springs from its biblical convictions. And it has to be said that in this morality shades of centre and right merge together. The agenda is very clear: the sanctity of life, heterosexual sex within marriage. Given the influence of the media, it has been very difficult to present these issues positively without appearing to be antagonistic to other people.

Yet all too often evangelical sermons, teaching and political action on these matters betray a lack of love and descend into language which fails to convey *good news* to the world. When we protest and campaign on these issues, people are simply not believing us when we say that we love them. And they are finding it inconceivable that God loves them either. The evangelical public voice rallies the troops, builds platforms and even helps raise cash – financial supporters and partners from the centre and right are easily motivated by these issues. But the world has not been convinced by our moral message, which has done nothing to make Christ credible in the public square.

If more evangelicals on the right spent half of their budgets and energies devising creative ways in which to talk up good news and presenting Christ, then people might be better able to hear their arguements.

So what are we to do? Abandon our positions on these key moral issues? Absolutely not. But in our liberal democracies the new option may be to state our case clearly and then simply leave it visible in the public square. We must give ourselves permission to stop shouting about it at every given opportunity and to talk about other things as well.

What of politics on the evangelical right? Very often the political right of evangelicalism relates comfortably to the centre. People have noticed that the evangelicals who speak out against gays do not go to rallies about the environment or campaign on global poverty. They have noticed that they are slower to be involved in community and still have theological arguements for non-engagement. As Simon Manchester put it: "You'll really be doing double back-flips to get a social programme out of Matthew 25."[3]

Of course all evangelicals have a responsibility to rehabilitate "evangelical" as good news. But if we are to succeed, those on the right have an urgent agenda to work through. A good deal of this must happen in the public sphere where most people have their encounters with evangelicals.

- We must rapidly widen our political discourse beyond a moral agenda to wider ethical debates. As far as morality is concerned, we have lost all the battles and we are losing the war. This is certainly true in the US where the Christian Coalition has failed to deliver on these issues – even with sustained periods of Republicanism. In a US national survey we learned that married couples are now the minority household, with 51 percent of women living alone for the first time in American history.[4] Similar trends are being seen in Europe. We must be faithful to our convictions on the moral agenda, but there is little point in shouting until people are ready to listen again.

  We must rapidly widen our political discourse beyond a moral agenda to wider ethical debates. As far as morality is concerned, we have lost all the battles and we are losing the war.

- We really must vet our language and letters which so badly misrepresent Christ. On one occasion a policy advisor told me that the most obnoxious letters regarding homosexuality were sent just as often by evangelical Christians as by the opposing gay lobby.

- Let's all give up the Moral Majority mind-set. I have never met a politician, journalist or member of the public who thinks Moral Majority is a synonym for Jesus Christ. We must leave behind an ethos which has failed politically and, worse still, has done nothing to present the church as good news to a world in search of it.

- Evangelicals on the right have become judgemental in the public square. Somehow we have to find better ways to help people understand that God is a God of judgement without becoming judgemental ourselves. "Effective evangelism that results in long-term good news," says Chris Wright, "does not have to include offensive and denunciatory attacks on other people's convictions (Acts 19:36)."[5] The kind of behavior which saw a prominent North American evangelical leader publicly advocate the assassination of President Chavez of Venezuela in 2005 is a serious liability to good news.

- Neither should evangelicals give uncritical support to Israel in its relationship with Palestinians. It is perfectly possible to believe – as many evangelicals do – that God has orchestrated the return of his people to Israel without unconditionally condoning injustice in Palestine. Evangelicals have a role to play in praying and advocating for a way forward which ensures both security for Israel and justice for Palestinians – of whom 1.5 million are Christians.

> Somehow we have to find better ways to help people understand that God is a God of judgement without becoming judgemental ourselves.

We must learn to mingle revelation, prophecy and political justice, and we are not always very good at it. We simply cannot turn a blind eye to injustice any more than Amos or Micah could. If we become uncritical friends of Israel, that is precisely what we do.

It is one thing to do trips to the Holy Land: I have benefited immensely from them. But it is quite another to stand by the security wall and to talk with our Palestinian brothers and sisters who suffer. No evangelical should visit Israel without listening to a Palestinian Christian. That is a serious neglect.

None of this is to understate the terrible pain that Israel has suffered from hostile neighbours bent on its destruction. This is no apology for the suicide bomber. But "evangelical" must never become a synonym for unqualified friendship with Israel. Our very commitment to God's purposes for his people insists that we urge them into righteousness.

- Finally, we must recognise that serving the community is more important than our minority rights. Losing our religious liberties is not the worst thing that could happen to Christians in post-Christendom; losing the right to serve is.

TO THE CENTRE

Evangelical categories are difficult. Who belongs precisely where is a very hard thing to agree on.

But just to make sense of this conversation, let's assume that by the "centre" I am referring to evangelicals who firmly believe in the central ideas about the Bible as God's inspired word to humankind; that Jesus is the final revelation of God; and that the congenital sin which separates us from him can only be dealt with by the atoning death of Jesus Christ. Such people may or may not be theologically Reformed.

They are likely to be mainstream charismatic and are unlikely to be influenced by more contemplative spiritualities even where these do not deny the atoning work of Christ. They have varying levels of involvement in prayer movements and spiritual warfare and are very open to charismatic gifts.

They share conservative values with those on the right and are quite attentive to the moral concerns around human sexuality, abortion and family issues. They agree that social engagement is important and are increasingly politically aware and active in the community. They are less motivated by issues of global poverty or injustice, and some may even tolerate or strongly advocate prosperity preaching.

People in the centre generally flow with prescriptive forms of gathered church structure and may find themselves more uneasy with fresh or emerging expressions. They are unlikely to be monastic. With few exceptions they will work ecumenically but are less comfortable in multi-faith settings. They are cautiously inclusive. They are not always sensitive about culture and how evangelicals come across to the world. They are quite diverse in their attitudes to women bishops and pastors and may not approve if you miss the Sunday service to go to the cinema instead!

They are often impatient with those people who they feel give evangelicals a bad name by protests, ungracious attitudes and stodgy doctrines.

They carry a left-right gene.

They're likely to be over fifty but there are plenty of thirty-somethings too. Invariably they are happy to hold to the "evangelical" label.

Now everyone reading this will know someone who claims to be centre but for whom these categories do not apply! But I did say it was difficult.

The word "evangelical" is guaranteed for the foreseeable future largely because of centre people.

> The word "evangelical" is guaranteed for the foreseeable future largely because of centre people.

In general, centre evangelicals are happy to flow with the view that Christians have a role to play in community and political affairs. This is quite different from party-political allegiance. No alliance of evangelicals would formally attach itself to any political party, but all alliances actively seek out or are open to partnership and dialogue with politicians and policy makers. The nervousness about political engagement which muzzled the evangelical voice for over three decades was finally ended by the conscious commitments of evangelical leaders at the Lausanne Congress in 1974. Since that time there have been few in the centre who would consciously avoid political or community engagement.

But this engagement is not actually as novel as we make it sound. It has in fact been generally central to evangelicalism for two hundred years or more. "Evangelical" will be redefined as good news to the extent that the church once again embraces its mission as hope-bringer in every aspect of community life. Social action integral to evangelical witness is likely to help our world realise that gospel people are good news people. It would be unwise to single out individuals who have influenced our thinking in this regard, but it seems that one exception needs to be made: John Stott.[1] A *New York Times* article in 2005 described him as the "Archbishop of Evangelicalism". Largely as a result of his writings, it is now commonplace to find prominent Christian leaders across the world promoting social action both in their native lands and overseas. And many of these leaders do so in partnerships with governments with whom they have personal relationships.

When evangelicals deliver multi-million dollar relief and development projects or feed the hungry in their neighborhoods, they become good news.

In October 2006, I sat under a blazing sun in the Watoto Children's Village in Suubi, Uganda. Along with two thousand others, I listened to Mother Maggi's account of how the project had changed her life. Now fifty-six, she was one of the mothers caring for over 560 Ugandan children orphaned by AIDS. Along with her three children, she had become an outcast when her husband died of the disease and she herself was diagnosed HIV positive. Her relatives called her family "walking corpses". Now here she was on a hill overlooking Kampala promising to raise up a thousand future leaders for

Uganda and telling us: "We are no longer walking corpses but blessed."

This is the good news which should become synonymous with evangelical.

Centre evangelicals have the capacity to cast a swing vote on the public performances of their leaders and representatives. Generally they are tolerant of those who walk on the foundation stones of evangelical faith but who are prepared to sometimes take chances in the public square. They are like the weathercocks which swivel around in the wind but stay firmly attached to the church tower. People in the centre will still hear truth in the context of relationships. They have an amazing ability to be both fixed in their ways yet open to possibilities.

Even if they are uncomfortable with ecumenical relationships, they will generally give permission for others to explore and sometimes join the expedition. They will cherry-pick from right and left viewpoints, testing and discerning them in the context of their own personal reading and favourite Christian media programmes. But generally they never promote personalities above their own biblical convictions. However much they love you, they will switch you off if you keep getting it wrong!

But if you push them on moral and theological issues, they are conservatively right and even reactionary. They hold fast to the old agendas. They may vote Labour or Christian Socialist in Europe, or Democrat in the US, but this has no bearing on their moral vote. Homosexual practice, abortion and extramarital sex are wrong. Even if they come from broken families, they defend family life. Gambling and swearing are generally off-limits.

And they are not afraid to tell other people that they think these things are important. Centre people have the capacity to be mobilised by – or at least supportive of – public campaigns promoting these moral imperatives.

> Generally, centre evangelicals never promote personalities above their own biblical convictions. However much they love you, they will switch you off if you keep getting it wrong!

And they value the church. For many of them – particularly the over-fifties – it is their life. Their moral and theological reticence holds them back from spiritual revolutions, but they don't necessarily like to stand still either. So church life needs to be predictably progressive or else they get bored. Many have left evangelical churches to have their brains stimulated elsewhere. Generally they have a high tolerance level for what goes on inside the church, but they have also lost their denominational loyalties. Many of them are on their third or forth stop from Brethren to Baptist to Episcopalian to Pentecostal to independent charismatic to Methodist to staying at home and starting over again! These are eclectic evangelicals.

But more than anything else they are theologically cautious, vehemently defending historic positions on the virgin birth, biblical inspiration and the cross. Mainstream, centre evangelicalism has come a long way from the anti-intellectualism of the 1900s. It is packed with good scholarship and self-taught preachers whose more recent Pentecostal and charismatic insights have made very important contributions to evangelical belief. But evangelicals in the centre also don't need a PhD in a specific area to express strong opinions on it – just listen to any Christian phone-in program! They won't shrug their shoulders and walk away from a topic just because they haven't been to Bible college.

The evangelical centre, which holds in tension the dynamics of right and left, has a critical role to play in rehabilitating evangelical as good news. It has no right to define what evangelical means any more than those on the left or right. But it is precisely at the fulcrum of left and right that people will understand the gospel as a good news message.

It is here that twenty-first century evangelicals can be converted into active citizens who, for example, work through the complications of rights and equalities. They are waiting to be taught how to live skilfully in palaces without selling their souls to the culture.[2] If evangelical leaders put their minds to it, these people could be taught the fine art of Christian compromise – being as wise as serpents but as harmless as doves.[3]

They love the idea of church. They can be committed to agitate for change without abandoning the idea of a gathered congregation. But at the same time they are generally flexible enough to salute fresh expressions and emerging church without condemnation. The problem at the centre is a lack of courageous leaders who will help people shift from attending church to being good news.

The great news however is that this love for church has led to a growing confidence about its role in the world. It's not just mega-church leaders like Bill Hybels and Rick Warren who believe that "the church is the hope of the world". That idea has become infectious, and today thousands of local churches are caught up in world missions, nationwide and local social action and vibrant evangelism. Their left-right balance gives them the flexibility, the buildings and the infrastructure to be effective in this way.

People at the centre are not compromisers: they are the best hope of rehabilitating western evangelicals because, as

Philip Yancey noted, in many other parts of the world they are the ones communicating the good news: "When I return from trips and read profiles in *Time* and *Newsweek* about US evangelicals, I feel sad. Many Americans view evangelicals as a monolithic voting bloc obsessed with a few moral issues. They miss the vibrancy and enthusiasm, the 'good-news-ness' that the word 'evangelical' represents in much of the world."[4]

A GOOD NEWS AFTERTHOUGHT

When I first raised the notion that the word "evangelical" should be rehabilitated as "good news", it provoked a lot of discussion among friends, staff and the Council of the Evangelical Alliance UK. Most people were quite excited about the idea while others wondered if it could ever be done. Many said it would be extremely difficult. But very few said it *should not* be done. Because "evangelical" *means* good news, and because people outside the church need good news, we have a duty to try.

My facile left, centre and right categories were broad generalizations to help us respond to some evangelical realities if we are to be known as good news. The relationship between the positions is a finely tuned synergy. Generally we are to the right on moral issues and centrist to left on socio-political agendas. The tension which results in an intelligent centre is based to some extent on how both left and right react and respond to each other.

There is no doubt that evangelicalism is a complicated family. But we are all in it together.

Unity is therefore central.[1] There is a view that says that some evangelicals put unity *above* biblical truth and will make any compromise to look united. But this is in fact a very unbiblical view because unity itself is a biblical truth.[2] And

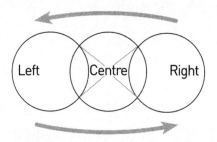

that unity is based first and foremost on our faith in God, our relationship to Jesus Christ through the forgiveness of sin and our commitment to the truth and authority of his word.[3] Biblical truth is both personal and propositional.

Our unity should not be judged on whether we all agree to do the same things in the same way. Our methods should not separate us. Although we need the agitation of "progressive" evangelicals, they must also recognize their need for everybody else if they are to avoid overdosing on novelty. And we need the anchor of our conservatives as long as they recognise that anchors can be a problem when you want to get under way. The middle ground holds our unity together when evangelical civil wars take place.

> Although we need the agitation of "progressive" evangelicals, they must also recognize their need for everybody else if they are to avoid overdosing on novelty.

We should all be able to agree that good news is about the gospel and that proclamation is certainly not about telling the world that God is an uncritical best friend and they have nothing to worry about! As Martin Luther once said, we must know God as an enemy before we know him as a friend. Evangelicals will always say that the good news of the gospel begins with repentance.[4] But it doesn't end there. God has always been generous to sinners and so should we be. If our posture is one of good news, people may hear us better when we speak about their sins. Jesus touched and taught the people as he brought them to repentance.[5]

If we want to be considered as good news in the world, *we* have the power to make it happen. This is not to say that the media, which thrives on confrontation, will not be an enormous obstacle to overcome. But the alternative is not to avoid the press. In a media-driven world, that is a lazy luxury we cannot afford. We must learn to win by wooing. We must learn to show *anguish* more than *anger*. People must know we care about the pain they feel. This was a sentiment very much expressed by the late, great Francis Schaeffer, "a rare Christian leader who advocated understanding and empathising with non-Christians instead of taking issue with them".[6]

> We must learn to win by wooing. We must learn to show *anguish* more than *anger*. People must know we care about the pain they feel.

And if we are to be good news, people should identify us not with our campaigns or concerns but with Jesus himself. If evangelicals fail in this they fail in their mission. That mission is not to win political points in the public square; it is to present Christ as a credible Saviour to society, and we should be unmistakably identified with him. That is why pagans first called the church "Christians". The gospel is bound to Jesus Christ. It is the good news about him.[7] We must not allow the word "evangelical" to stand in the way of the word "gospel" and block people from seeing Jesus Christ.

Even if evangelical cannot be rehabilitated as good news, we should be happy to die trying! And if it's true that evangelicals make up 6.5 percent of the world's population,[8] think what might happen across the world if 20 percent of evangelical churches asked themselves two important questions: *What does it mean to be good news?* and *What does it mean to act out good news?*

On a wall in Pip & Jay – an Anglican church in Bristol – there is a plaque which reads:

Mrs Ann Baskerfield of Leighton in the County of Bedford Who died in Bristol 1st May 1802 aged 50 years.

Her Chief Delight was in Doing Good.

PART 3

ENGAGING IN SPIRITUAL AND
SOCIAL TRANSFORMATION

> *Likewise anyone with this God-*
> *link to the Liberator is a brand*
> *new human being; not genetically*
> *modified – brand new! The old*
> *categories don't work; it's a whole*
> *new ballgame.*
>
> —2 Cor 5:17 (The Word on the Street)

If the good news of evangelical faith does not result in transformation then it is not good news. If it does not turn the lives of individuals and communities on their heads then the kingdom of God has not truly broken in. If our salt is not flavoring the whole batch then what sort of salt is it?

Transformation is the inevitable result of incarnation. Nobody who had a meaningful contact with Jesus was ever the same again. But this transformational impact was not just limited to individuals. Society itself was changed. Jesus stepped into a Roman empire that had a casual and selective respect for human life and told Jews and Gentiles alike that the very hairs on their head were numbered by the Father. He changed the rules. He changed the values.

As God's incarnation in the twenty-first century, the church is called to have the same transformational impact: life by life and culture by culture. We are called to model a better way more than we are called to criticise the existing one. We are called to be the solution we want to see in the midst of the moral and social fragmentation of western societies. We are called to measure our effectiveness not by the size of our churches but by their impact on our communities and the radical discipleship of their members.

It is a long-term mission, and it may be that we only lay the foundations for future generations. But it is a vital one. And our gasping cultures cannot afford for us to neglect it.

GOD'S GONE PUBLIC

In the early twentieth century, evangelicals bought a late nineteenth-century lie. The lie was that religion should be privatised and that God wasn't that bothered about social engagement. Social action was left to liberal Christians and historic older denominations like Catholics, Anglicans, Presbyterians and Salvationists. As social action became seen as a new kind of salvation, the evangelicals retreated from what became known as the social gospel.

In the 1970s much of that began to change as evangelicals saw that social engagement was a complement rather than a contradiction to good news. As Alistair McGrath put it: "The social gospel got one thing right and everything else wrong. 'What God has joined together let no man put asunder.'"[1]

Evangelicals of all shades are now involved in public life. Even where they are weak on community involvement they are likely to be actively lobbying government on legislation affecting the nation's morality.

The dichotomy is dying. We can no longer separate our spiritual lives from our involvement in the world. And because of this, the idea of transformation has become very popular amongst evangelicals.

So what is transformation?

The dichotomy is dying. We can no longer separate our spiritual lives from our involvement in the world.

Evangelicals are not social engineers. We do not believe that change takes place merely by altering social conditions. Biblical transformation begins with a personal encounter with God because Jesus has forgiven our sins. In fact, the fuel of historic evangelical missions and social reforms was usually evangelism. Evangelical transformation in the eighteenth and nineteenth centuries sprung from a hatred of sin and what it does to people. As the historian John Wolffe said: "Social transformation must be seen as part and parcel of evangelism not as an alternative to it."[2]

But personal salvation is just the starting point.

A Christianity which does not begin with the individual will never begin. But likewise a Christianity which ends with the individual will soon end.[3]

This is God's bigger agenda in transformation. From the fall in Genesis to the inevitable triumph of Christ in Revelation, God has shown himself to be committed to changing people and things. Evangelicals join with that commitment.

But transformation is not utopianism and does not oblige us to any particular millennial position.

A Christian view of transformation does not pretend that we can create perfect societies through our work. But it imagines a society in which our prayers and efforts mean that more people will come to faith in Jesus Christ and that God's kingdom of justice will inch its way deeper into our fallen relationships, promoting justice and human flourishing.

It is a transformation that means that "some will get saved but everyone will benefit".[4]

If we are to achieve this we need to think differently about ourselves. We need to think of ourselves not just as individual disciples, church members, prayer warriors or even good evangelists. We need to think of ourselves as Christian citizens refreshed and commissioned by the church to do the work of the kingdom.

Transformation then is not an added extra which we elect into. It is the sum total of what God is doing in the world and what he invites us to join in with.[5] Historically, evangelicalism is unrecognisable without

> A Christian view of transformation means that "some will get saved but everyone will benefit".

it. It is the mission mind-set without which we fail ourselves and society. In its absence we fold in on ourselves, splitting theological hairs and propping up structures designed to keep us safe from the world. It's like fire officers discussing interior design while the city burns.

Making a difference – liberating captives – should be the hallmark of every evangelical congregation. It's far more important than who's in the choir or what the departmental budgets look like.

Transformation enforces hope. It is what is needed in our town halls, community projects and parliaments. As Jim Wallis points out: "Hope versus cynicism is the key moral and political choice of our time."[6] We really shouldn't underestimate this. When I spoke to a senior police officer in the West Midlands some years ago, he told me how in his patch a young man could be killed in a night-club simply because he appeared to disrespect another person. I asked him what it was which drove young people to such madness. His answer came very swiftly: a lack of hope.

Transforming hope is the joy of a local pastor who leads the unbelieving husband of a faithful member to Christ. It is the giving of Communion to someone in their dying moments. But it is also shown in a thousand other ways. In recent years

I have had the privilege of visiting Africa with Tearfund and India with World Vision and have seen hope in action. Hope is a cow in a field; it's a fishing boat after a tsunami; it's a red tractor shared between several families. Hope is practical. It's God's way of saying that tomorrow is possible and that he is everybody's God.

Evangelicals committed to spiritual and social transformation will not be known for who or what they are against. They will be known for what they are for: pro-community based on kingdom values. Evangelicalism is true to itself when it makes positive contributions to its world. That's what good news does.[7]

We must never think that our transformational work goes unobserved. The new evangelical engagement has been duly noted. There is a very good reason why political leaders are falling over themselves to work with faith groups and churches. As former Prime Minister Tony Blair said in a celebration walkabout after his historic victory in 1997: "We will work with anyone who can deliver the goods!" Evangelical transformation steps out of the building to "deliver the goods".

Making a difference – liberating captives – should be the hallmark of every evangelical congregation. It's far more important than who's in the choir or what the departmental budgets look like.

Evangelical engagement in the US has been noted by people of very different faiths. In September 2005, *Christianity Today* posted an excellent article by a Jewish human rights activist who said that evangelicals had quietly become "the most powerful force for human-rights progress".[8]

Across Africa, Sri Lanka, India – to name a few – evangelicals are actively involved in human rights and religious liberties. In its eighteenth-century heyday the Evangelical Alliance UK was known as a champion of religious liberties. Today the World

Evangelical Alliance's Religious Liberties Commission has formal status at the United Nations.

At the close of the twentieth century, evangelicals found themselves at the heart of the world's greatest and most sustained campaign against poverty. Jubilee Campaign drew world-class celebrities such as Bono and Bob Geldof as champions, but it began as the vision of a staff member at Tearfund UK. That commitment has been sustained and developed in evangelical involvement in Make Poverty History.

Since its formal launch at the United Nations in 2004, Micah Challenge has emerged as a significant evangelical response to world poverty, calling governments to account on their progress on the Millennium Development Goals (MDGs) – eight promises by which they have agreed to reduce extreme poverty by 50 percent by 2015. By deepening our commitment to the poor and advocating with them, the global evangelical community has agreed to become a critical partner with national governments in delivering these promises.

When I visited the United Nations Development Programme in Nairobi, which has responsibility for implementation of the MDGs across Africa, a national coordinator told me, "If the church in Africa develops Micah Challenge, my work will be reduced by half!" Micah Challenge is recognised not only at the United Nations but also by Global Call to Action Against Poverty (GCAP) for its unique response to global poverty and its growing partnership with governments in poverty reduction.

Micah Challenge is an amazing opening for positive prophetic evangelicalism which makes sense to the twenty-first century.[9]

If transforming lives and communities became the arrowhead of the local church, it would have a profound effect on all that we do.

How might it affect our worship and preaching?

What would it mean for our youth programs and outreach?

What messages would we want people to go out with as they left our buildings? And would they leave feeling confident about their role in society or anxious about surviving until the next Sunday service?

What, for example, would we describe as our priorities in time, human resources and budgets?

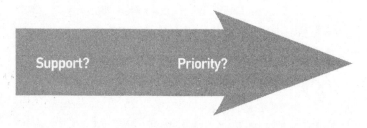

These are large-scale responses to transformational work. But every local congregation should become an agent of change, taking responsibility for the square mile around its building and teaching its members to do the same where they live.

God has gone public. But people will only know if we are there to show them.

TOWARDS EVANGELICAL CITIZENS

Discipleship is one of those important subjects which evangelical leaders know they must talk about and which the people know they should listen to. The only problem is that many people are still struggling to apply what they know about it.

It's true that Jesus sent out twelve disciple-makers into the world. But sadly, so much of our contemporary approach to discipleship locks us into personal piety issues. It may improve our relationship with God, get us to read our Bibles and pray more earnestly, but usually it does nothing to lead us into a transforming mind-set. The truth is that real biblical discipleship is inherently transformational, in any culture and at any time.[1] In the book of Acts, disciples were people learning their craft in the rough and tumble of their communities, changing and challenging them at every turn. Somehow we have allowed it to become no more than a series of systems and programmes locked into the local church.

A good citizen is involved with what is happening around her in the lives of people in her local community. Even if she was born on the other side of the world, her zip code and tax demand mean that she is one of them!

In the book of Acts, disciples were people learning their craft in the rough and tumble of their communities, changing and challenging them at every turn. Somehow we have allowed it to become no more than a series of systems and programmes locked into the local church.

We work and worship within the community. This is what Miroslav Volf thinks: "Christian difference is therefore not an insertion of something new into the old from outside, but the bursting out of the new precisely within the space of the old."[2]

Good news is moved to act in the midst of bad news.

Some years ago I sat in my car with my teenage children chomping through a McDonald's take-away. Passengers in a car next to us, and parked by a rubbish bin, began to throw rubbish out the window onto the ground. I was incensed and wondered what kind of people could do such things! But I also felt an amazing prompting to go out and clear it up. I was as amazed by my actions as my children. Something had said: "You are a part of this mess. Don't complain about it; help clear it up."

Evangelical citizens know that serving the common good is more important than defending Christian rights. They will argue for their basic rights as citizens, as Paul did,[3] but beyond this their real passion has nothing to do with screaming for "their rights" in the public square. That's what everybody else does. It has to do with leading people to the kingdom and serving communities. If people catch us on a protest, there should be a good chance that we are marching for someone else's rights.

If people catch us on a protest, there should be a good chance that we are marching for someone else's rights.

The idea of citizenship responsibility has always been at the heart of spiritual engagement with political systems. Daniel the Jew was faultless as a Babylonian citizen, so they trapped him on the basis of his faith.[4] When Jesus was brought before Pilate, Pilate's primary concern was to test his citizenship: was he for or against Rome? What tipped the scales against Jesus was not what he said about being God's son but the fact that the Jews made him out to be anti-Caesar.[5] And the same was true for the early church which fought constantly to demonstrate that Christian faith made them salt and light in society.

One of the greatest arguements for the existence of the early church was not only that God was on its side but that the Christians were on the side of their society. Kill us, they said, and you kill your very best citizens!

A citizenship mind-set is pre-occupied not with its own safety but with the well-being of its community. Evangelical citizens do not argue primarily for religious rights; they argue for freedom for all people *and within that* freedom to practice faith. In the early church the Parabolani was a special team of Christians which served the community – sometimes at the cost of their own lives. In fact Parabolani means "to expose oneself to danger". In public gatherings they were illegal, but "they did take part in public life."[6]

Charles Colson puts it like this: "Our job is not only to build up the church but also to build society to the glory of God."[7]

What seems evident from the history of evangelical public engagement in Britain is that people often come to be followers of Christ not *only* as a direct result of evangelism but also as a result of the church's involvement in the real issues of the day.

> A citizenship mind-set is pre-occupied not with its own safety but with the well-being of its community.

The pre-occupation of the church with mission caused the church to be shaped around mission and so to become an effective means of transforming both individuals and society as a genuine people movement. No one engaged in a campaign to abolish slavery in order to boost church attendance, yet paradoxically, by engaging first and foremost in mission, the fortunes of the church were transformed.[8]

Discourse is crucial. Jesus, Paul, the apostles and the early church all recognised the value of meaningful discourse with the authorities. Even under pre-Constantinian persecution, Christian leaders engaged in correspondence with their Roman persecutors. The tone of many of the epistles (particularly Romans and 1–2 Peter) is all about building witnessing lifestyles and engaging in dialogue with pagan neighbours.

Christian citizenship means that we will never be satisfied with raising our voice in anger without offering some good advice as well. Out of captivity both Joseph and Daniel came to prominence because they had useful things to say about the big problems of their day. Jim Wallis is right to remind us that protest is not enough.[9] If people know we are with them, they will still know we are for them when we disagree.

So here is what Pulitzer Prize-winning journalist Nicholas Kristof had to say when the National Association of Evangelicals in America published its *Evangelical Call to Civic Responsibility*: "The National Association of Evangelicals has re-branded the movement as a group of people who are trying desperately to alleviate human suffering."[10]

Christian citizenship really isn't selling our souls; it's recovering the core of our being. And when we do, we become more recognisable to a watching world.

The idea that a local church can become so embroiled in its community that it makes a real difference is catching on; we must fan the flames.

> Christian citizenship really isn't selling our souls; it's recovering the core of our being. And when we do, we become more recognisable to a watching world.

Now let me tell you about a church in the heart of London. It has a leadership team of three. Two are full-time and the third is a part-time teacher. She is committed to staying in education as she says that educating children in schools is in fact her primary calling.

Visitors are welcome, but everyone who is formally linked to the church is assigned to a personal coach in the local congregation. This relationship is designed not to suffocate but to guide its "members" in a personal dialogue about life in community. Every person is asked to take on one voluntary commitment in the local community where they live, and this commitment is regarded as their primary reason for being together as a worshipping community. Their weekly bulletin has basic advice on things like energy conservation in the home. They have a slogan on it which says, "You're only in when you're out" (Acts 1:8).

At any one time only two-fifths of its activities will have an internal focus. It consciously avoids departmental activities such as women's and men's ministries. It does not have weekly prayer meetings. It seeks instead to instil these Christian habits in its members' orientation. It has block periods of specially focused prayer and events which deal with matters of intimacy which may not be appropriate in the normal teaching programme.

The church jealously restricts the volume of internal activities to teaching, worship and caring. Its worship is vibrant and open to spiritual gifts to provide insights into strategic mission beyond the building. There is room for the feel-good factor in worship, but the leadership is keen to ensure that its citizenship ethos is not displaced by this. The preaching varies between forty-minute sermons and fifteen-minute exhortations with topical interviews to underscore the subject. It is also typical to have engaging input from local politicians, councillors, police and community leaders on issues relating to the square mile around the church. Local civic leaders are constantly mentioned or prayed for by name in the worship service. While it is slightly controversial, occasionally the church asks a leader of another faith to address them in their Sunday morning setting. These services are usually organised sensitively to avoid the impression of multi-faith worship. Visitors will often respond to questions from the congregation about their faith.

The youth and children's work has been developed as an extension of the school week. Children and young people are helped to understand the Bible and what it means for them in their encounters with people of other faiths. They are also used to seeing their schoolteachers as occasional visitors to their church. The issues dealt with in the children's "Little Ask" & "Big Ask!" youth programs deal with subjects such as bullying, addiction, solvent abuse and sex from a Christian perspective. Much of this material, though based on Christian values, is geared to the diverse community, and the church often issues invitations to children and parents outside the church who might be coming along. One parent said: "I knew it was religious, but it was dealing with the stuff I was telling my kids about last week when we were watching TV."

The teaching for youth and young adults in their twenties and thirties will often examine contemporary films or TV series from a Christian perspective. A recent topic was "How user-friendly is *Friends*?" The discussion was conducted by two professional Christian actors.

The church has not experienced dramatic growth, but there is a steady stream of new arrivals – mainly local people who are finding faith and a spiritual home. It has grown from 243 to 296 over a fifteen-month period, and the indications are that the rate of growth is increasing.

Actually I don't know of such a church, but I imagine it exists.

30% OFF

all canvas wraps

Ask in-store for details

JESSOPS

YOUR PICTURES. OUR PASSION.

IN FOR THE LONG HAUL

In the autumn of 2006 I spent a weekend in the English town of Salisbury and had the Saturday free. I promised that I would treat myself to a day in the cathedral. It was my second time in the building. Two years earlier I had preached there on a Harvest Sunday. At the time I hadn't really taken much notice of my surroundings: it was strictly business. But on this occasion the visit was just for me and I loved it.

Salisbury is one of the oldest and most historically important cathedrals in Britain. It is home to the famous Magna Carta of 1215 AD which laid out the agreement between the king and the barons, and was effectively the first piece of written constitutional law in the United Kingdom. Another display shows the elaborate plans for the construction of the building which took over forty years to put up. I marvelled at these intricate plans for some time, and as I did so a number of things struck me quite deeply.

Firstly was the intentionality behind the building. You simply don't just get up one morning and decide to build yourself a cathedral! Everything has to come together: a labor force, finances and building materials. In a period when life expectancy did not exceed the mid-thirties, very few of the workmen who began the project were likely to see the finished product. For that matter, neither would the designer.

But cathedrals aren't just beautiful buildings. They are made to last. Over 1,200 years after its inception, as I wandered around on a busy Saturday afternoon, the cathedral was alive with tourists, swelled with the sound of a rehearsing choir, and generating some much-needed income in a thriving canteen and souvenir shop. And the building has a long history to tell. So much of the life of the district and the nation has been shaped by events here. The cathedral has contributed to and received from the political, social and even economic life of the land.

A few weeks later, as we were approaching Christmas, I happened to tune into the annual "Darkness and Light" service on the BBC which comes from Salisbury Cathedral. The choral festival attracts people from all over the world – a sell-out event which celebrates the season and draws locals and visitors into the spiritual life of the building. Over a millennium later we can still live, marvel and worship in the shadow of other people's long-term strategic thinking.

> You simply don't just get up one morning and decide to build yourself a cathedral!

God is a long-term thinker. Before the world began Jesus was already commissioned to atone for sins we had yet to commit. The entire Bible is a statement of intentionality. And in our personal programmes of transformation, God waits patiently with us as we grow more like Jesus. God's actions are always timely and in time. As the saying goes, "If something's worth doing, it's worth doing well."

Long-term intentional thinking is not the same as procrastination even though it may appear so to onlookers.

And long-term thinking does not always come easily to evangelicals. As Bebbington's definition suggests, evangelicals are activists.[1] We love things to happen "immediately". St Mark should be our patron saint.

But although activism is really important, strategic intent is also vital. Most of us are impatient with the sterile ploddings of academics and thinkers. We tire of talk. After all, we say, the church has been talking for two thousand years! Enough now! What is there new to say? There is much truth in this. As a Christian leader I have also had my fair share of talking. But we only "waste time talking" when we have already figured out what to do. So Leon Hynson warns that we should "avoid the impatience of an activism which is theologically sterile as well as a theology which belongs only in the classroom".[2]

Activism is our response to the immediate calamities facing us in the world. It plunges us in to grab as many drowning people as our energies allow: but it doesn't build lifeboats.

It secretes spiritual adrenalin, makes sense of our passions and appeals to our funders. But it doesn't bring change which lasts. Activism makes changes; strategic activity brings transformation. Activism changes people and their circumstances; strategic activity changes values and ultimately systems.

Not even great spiritual awakenings replace the importance of deliberate long-term thinking. Evangelicals put a great deal of store behind prayer gatherings targeted at government and policy-making. All of this is really critical because we are commanded to pray for our leaders. But it's important to remember that generally in the New Testament, prayers for government and leaders are prayers not solely for justice and peaceful leadership.

They are prayers that just and peaceful governments will lead to transformed societies.[3]

Not even great spiritual awakenings replace the importance of deliberate long-term thinking.

Revival is integral to the spring-cleaning work of God as he renews hope in succeeding generations. But it is no substitute for strategies for change which the Holy Spirit inspires in our hearts and relationships.

Revival reminds me of the man who complained to me that I had prayed for him and he ended up in the hospital. I told him that had I not prayed for him he would now be dead! Revival comes to our communities to "give us a chance". It's a snippet of heaven and a reminder that God still has our best interests at heart. But waiting for the revival that will change public life and society may be an abdication of our responsibility to work strategically with God to witness a sea-change in our culture.

A couple of examples:

- The Reformation was not an overnight wonder. It was the result of a series of rigorous theological reflections by a range of scholars in Europe. George Whitefield was said to be a greater preacher than Wesley. But Wesley's methods had a far more profound and lasting impact on world history.

- In the opening years of the twentieth century, one of the greatest revivals exploded in Los Angeles between 1903 and 1906. The result, as the first Pentecostal historian Frank Bartleman reported, was that "the colour line was washed away by the blood of Jesus." In the same period and in the same area, the black intellectual W. E. B. Du Bois said that the greatest challenge to face America in the twentieth century would be the question of race. Within a short period the colour line had reappeared in Los Angeles, and racism – more than anything else – rocked the young revival movement.

In the absence of Spirit-induced intentional thinking, neither evangelism nor even a pervasive Christian presence will guarantee a transformed society. It is perfectly possible to have a business filled with Christians, with a vibrant Christian fellowship, but to see no real transformational effect in the way the business is run. Collections of personal pietism on their own are not enough. Transformation has to be intentional.

The same is true for entire nations. In Uganda, 65 percent of the population attend church on a regular basis. But when a crucial mayoral election took place in Kampala in 2005, a Muslim with a questionable reputation was elected. In Jamaica over 65 percent of the population go to church every week, but between 1 – 4 January 2007,[4] there were twenty-six homicides. And this in a "Christian nation" of under three million people, with a newly appointed Christian prime minister eager for strategic responses to the needs of Jamaica. In too many parts of the world, high church attendance is co-existing with all the hallmarks of social, economic and cultural malaise – be it corruption, injustice or poverty.

Evangelicals who are hungry for transformation must work together to do four things: pray for God's revival, evangelise our nations, be actively involved and act strategically.

The challenge of our post-Christendom culture must be tackled as though our nations were never Christianised: we must think like a minority because that is what we have become. People who know the odds are stacked against them are more intentional about the battle. If

Evangelicals who are hungry for transformation must work together to do four things: pray for God's revival, evangelise our nations, be actively involved and act strategically.

we are to tackle secularisation or aggressive Islam, it will need to be prayed and thought through intentionally.

Perhaps if we thought about things a lot more, we might need to pray against some people a lot less.

Now is the time for prayerful and prophetic gatherings to build some modern cathedrals. These would be settings in which Christians identify strategies to impact education, business, the media, arts, politics, sport and technology – areas with such dramatic impacts on our culture. This is precisely what William Wilberforce and his colleagues did. They knew that in order to change legislation, they had to change values. Their chief purpose in life was to make goodness fashionable, and it wasn't until they had worked diligently for thirty years that the slave trade was abolished in 1807.

But, for a number of reasons, strategic work is all very hard. If we are to do it well, several things must change for evangelicals.

- We must think in less egotistic terms. Like the cathedral architects, more of us have to be prepared to lay down foundations without ever seeing the walls go up. We have to think about our children's children.
- Churches must adopt much more robust citizenship mind-sets. If we are concerned about the rise of militant Islam in our liberal democracies, agitation and aggressive prayers against Muslim people will do little for our case. In many ways Muslims are far better strategic thinkers. They tend to be far more intentional in their engagement in politics and business, demonstrating, for example, a commitment to change the education and banking systems. Our strategy should be one of assertive love and pervasive service. Think what might happen if every local church intentionally prayed for people who were openly placed on every local council, housing

association, youth service and within the criminal justice system.

- Most of us would agree that education, media, business, the arts, politics, technology and sports exert enormous influence on our culture. Imagine what might happen if there was a strategic, prayerful forum in every nation which thought carefully about how Christians work together to make well-being fashionable in each of these areas? In all of these influential places Christians exist, often without any support from their local churches. They show up to work in order to exist as a worker rather than operate as agents of change. If Christians in these places are ill-equipped to be transformers, where else will our culture be changed?

- And funders also need to be challenged. Christian foundations and philanthropists are – for very good reasons – being driven by commercial principles: they will put money where they see a return in the shortest possible time. Or they will give to high-profile activities. But they would have been unlikely to back Noah's ark or Wilberforce's campaign. Intentional transformation means casting our bread on the water.

Transformation is God's idea and long-term plan, but he has asked us to be part of it. As the historian David Bebbington reminds us: "Pondering their history may well lead evangelicals to prefer the slower and less spectacular methods that have reaped such rewards in the past. That is the way to root the gospel in our culture."[5]

In September 2000 the Evangelical Alliance UK put forward a vision of an Alliance working together as a movement for change. Our Council embraced it fully, and there were many enthusiastic responses from our members. Only one came back from an entire family. It said this:

Dear Joel and all working with EA,

We just wanted to add a small personal note with our cheque and reply form to say how encouraged we feel about EA's "movement for change". We feel privileged to be a part of this organisation.

Many thanks to you all for your hard work and commitment. We look forward to hearing news from you in the future.

Every blessing,
Tim and Rachel Jones
and also on behalf of our children:
Hannah age 6 (nearly 7)
Samuel age 5
Bethany age 3

I often think of this family when I think about the cathedral we are all building together.

QUESTIONS FOR DISCUSSION
AND RESPONSE

Chapter 1: Will the Real Jesus Step Forward?

1. Christ raised a question about his identity with his disciples near Caesarea Philippi. If Christ were to come to your town and ask people who they think he is, what kinds of answers do you think he might hear?

2. Why are questions about Jesus' identity more than academic conversations – making them hard to ignore?

3. The author describes the balance between the humanity and the deity of Jesus. He says: "Any portrait which loses this balanced mystery is a forgery." What do you think he means and do you agree?

4. The author asks: "How then has this life-giving and utterly generous Christ become so unrecognisably domesticated by evangelicals? How have we presented him as so risk-averse and timid that we often marginalise him from the people he came to live and die for?" Can you give some possible answers to these questions?

5. What are some ways you can grow in your understanding and appreciation of the real Christ and peel away possible layers of distortions that come from your subculture?

Chapter 2: Christ among the Gods

1. The author says: "Talk of ecumenism is old hat; the new debate is about inter-faith dialogue. It is now virtually impossible to find any community insulated from discussions about religion." What do you think? On a national level as well as on a local level, are discussions about Christianity and other religions occurring? Where? What are some examples?

2. What do you think of the contemporary pressures insisting on religious "sameness" to mirror the current cultural climate? How is this impacting the church? How should we respond to this pressure to play down differences among religions?

3. Is Jesus just different from other religious figures or is he superior? How would you express your convictions on this to people who are outside of the Christian faith?

4. What are the author's four suggestions on how to present Christ credibly to a pluralistic world? Do you agree or disagree with him on these?

5. What are some of the ways in which Christ is unique as compared to other gods?

Chapter 3: Rumours of Angels

1. What problem does the author have with miracles? Do you agree or disagree?

2. The author refers to many Bible-believing Christians being decidedly uncomfortable with the miraculous.

Do you think this is true among the Christians you know? If so, why?

3. The author says: "Our rational arguements are only a part of what makes the Bible believable. Ultimately the credibility of the Bible is in fact its incredulity." What do you think he means? Do you agree or disagree? Why?

4. The author asserts that "Christians who deny the place of miracles may wake up to find that we are out of step with contemporary culture growing weary with 'reason' which changes nothing and no one." Do you think contemporary culture is growing weary of reason? Can you think of any examples? What implications does this have for your church?

5. Do you think there's any correlation between the growth of Pentecostalism and its claims about miracles? Do you have any concerns about this growth?

Chapter 4: Christ the Conversationalist

1. Have you ever met someone so filled with the rightness of their own position that they were incapable of accommodating another point of view? Why do people become like this? How can Christians avoid this kind of attitude?

2. Do you think Christians feel fearful about anything in contemporary culture? What would be some examples? Why do some feel fearful? What counsel could you give them?

3. What can we learn from Jesus on how to relate to other people?

4. The author asserts: "The challenge of our day is to get involved in the conversations of our times in order to bring godly perspectives to the debate." How can we go about doing this? What do we have to offer to people?

5. What do you think the author means by conversational evangelicalism? Can you give any examples?

Chapter 5: Rock Steady

1. What is the main task of the church according to this chapter? What do you think of this understanding?
2. What is the issue of biblicism, and what does it mean to biblicise the church? What could you do in your church to see this happen?
3. What does it mean to have a church which behaves intelligently? How does your church rate?
4. Have evangelicals in the past put more emphasis on sexual ethics than on ethical responsibility in the social arena such as business conduct, responding to the poor and caring for the environment? If so, why has this happened? What can be done to restore balance?
5. What examples does the author give of ways Christians can increase their credibility with the world?

Chapter 6: What's in a Name?

1. If you interviewed a cross-section of people in your town and asked what they thought the word "evangelical" means, what do you think you might hear?
2. The author writes: "No one evangelical subculture has the right to decide what an evangelical is. Evangelical identity should be shaped by cultural blenders which work within the constellation of orthodox faith. It should be biblically solid at the core but culturally flexible on the edges." What do you think he means? Do you agree or disagree? What are some examples of being flexible on the edge?

3. What do you think of the idea that orthodoxy will always be bigger than evangelicalism? Is this a dangerous idea or one with which you are comfortable? Why?

4. Have you seen any examples of what the chapter called the doctrine of "guilt by association"? What are some problems with this?

5. What are Bebbington and Stott's understandings of "evangelicalism"? Do you feel closer to either of these understandings, or would you formulate a different definition?

Chapter 7: A Good Time to Be Good (News)

1. Why do you think a number of evangelicals are seeking to abandon the label "evangelical"? What do you think of the label?

2. One alternative is to work to find a better name to describe the distinctives of evangelicalism. Have you heard of any alternative terms, or can you come up with some possibilities?

3. The author argues for stripping away the caricatures of "evangelicalism" and keeping the name. What are some of his reasons for choosing this alternative? Do you agree or disagree?

4. The chapter indicates that evangelicals represent a key growth area in global Christianity. Apart from the author's examples, can you think of any other evidence to support this claim? In your local area are evangelical churches the ones growing the fastest? If not, who is growing faster?

5. The author suggests that perhaps evangelicals are more bothered by the "evangelical" label than people who are not Christians but simply indifferent. What do you

think? How do you think unchurched people in your area view the term? What might we do to help improve people's perceptions of evangelicals?

Chapter 8: To the Left

1. How does this chapter define the Christian left? Do you agree or disagree with this description?
2. Why is the evangelical left nervous about the word "evangelical?"
3. How would you summarize the author's counsel to people on the left? Would you add any additional counsel?
4. Why do people on the left need people in the centre and people on the right?
5. Can you think of examples of Christians on the left making a valuable contribution to the church and broader community?

Chapter 9: To the Right

1. What is the author's characterization of those who are part of the religious right? What do you think of this description? Would you change anything?
2. What have been some positive contributions of Christians on the right?
3. The author indicates "all too often evangelical sermons, teaching and political action on these matters [moral issues] betray a lack of love and descend into language which fails to convey good news to the world." Is that a fair or inaccurate assessment? Can you give any examples?
4. The chapter indicates that while we must not abandon our position on key moral issues, we must give

ourselves permission to stop shouting about it at every given opportunity and talk about other things as well. Do you think this is a good idea? Why or why not? What other things should we be talking about?

5. Do you think evangelicals have been judgemental in the public square? How do we help people understand that God is a God of judgement without becoming judgemental ourselves?

Chapter 10: To the Centre

1. How would you describe the evangelical centre as contrasted with the left and right?

2. What are some examples of "good news" which should become synonymous with evangelicalism?

3. What do you think centrist evangelicals think of the church? Why have some left evangelical churches?

4. What do you think the author means in saying that the evangelical centre has a critical role to play in rehabilitating "evangelical" as good news?

5. Do you agree or disagree with the statement that "many Americans view evangelicals as a monolithic voting bloc obsessed with a few issues"? Why? What do people think in other parts of the world?

Chapter 11: A Good News Afterthought

1. Do progressive evangelicals and conservative evangelicals need each other? Why or why not?

2. What does the author say about the media and our relation to it? What advice would you give to Christians who have dealings with the news media?

3. The author says, "If we are to be good news, people should identify us not with our campaigns or concerns

but with Jesus himself." How could we make this happen in our local area? In our country?

4. Martin Luther is reported to have said that we must know God as an enemy before we know him as a friend. What insight does scripture give on this? What do you think of this idea?

5. How would you and your church answer these questions: What does it mean to be good news? What does it mean to act out good news?

Chapter 12: God's Gone Public

1. Do you agree that the dichotomy is dying and we no longer can separate our spiritual lives from our social involvement in the world? What are the dangers in separating the two? In joining the two? Why has this subject been controversial for some?

2. What do you think is meant by the assertion that for transformation to take place, we need to think of ourselves not just as individual disciples, church members and prayer warriors, but as Christian citizens refreshed and commissioned to do the work of the kingdom? What difference might this shift in thinking make in your church and community?

3. The author says: "Evangelical transformation steps out of the building to 'deliver the goods'." Are people in your area doing this? Can you give some examples?

4. Evangelicals should be known for what they are *for* rather than just for who and what they are against. What are some things evangelicals in your area are known for?

5. If transforming lives and communities becomes the norm for your church, how do you think it might

affect the worship, preaching, youth programmes and outreach? How might your priorities change?

Chapter 13: Towards Evangelical Citizens

1. Do you agree that much of our contemporary discipleship approaches lock us into personal piety issues rather than community transformation? Why? Can you give some examples?
2. How can we fan the flames with the idea that the local church can become so involved in its community that it makes a real difference?
3. How would you describe the London church that the author envisions in this chapter?
4. What similarities and differences do you see between that church and your church?
5. What is the most helpful insight you discovered in this chapter?

Chapter 14: In for the Long Haul

1. Salisbury Cathedral is a good example of long-term intentional thinking. What are some other examples? The chapter suggests that evangelicals tend to be activists rather than long-term strategic thinkers. Do you agree or disagree? Why?
2. The author says: "In too many parts of the world, high church attendance is co-existing with all the hallmarks of social, economic and cultural malaise – be it corruption, injustice or poverty." What do you think of that assessment? What are some examples? Why does this happen?
3. The author notes four things necessary for transformation: (1) pray for God's revival, (2) evangelise our

nations, (3) be actively involved, and (4) act strategically. Which of these activities comes easiest for you? Which comes hardest? How much of this is currently occurring in your church?

4. What does the chapter say about Muslim people? What can we learn from them? What should the church be doing about Islam?

5. As a result of reading this book, how has your thinking changed? What would you now like to do?

NOTES

Preface: Background Noise or a Great Transforming Enterprise?

1. "Europe a Riddle Wrapped in an Enigma," World Evangelical Alliance, vol. 3, no. 3, 2004.
2. Cardinal Murphy-O'Connor address to Catholic leaders, 2004.
3. Peter Brierley, "Tide Is Running Out," Christian Research Association (CRA) press launch. Peter is Executive Director of CRA UK, and Britain's leading Christian statistician.
4. Matt 16:13–20.
5. 1 Chron 12:32.
6. 2 Tim 3:5.

Part 1: Presenting Christ Credibly to the Twenty-First Century

1. Matt 3:17; Rom 1:4.

Chapter 1: Will the Real Jesus Step Forward?

1. Luke 2:49.
2. Matt 16:13, 16.
3. John 1:29, 36.
4. Matt 3:17.
5. Acts 2:22, 36; Rom 1:4.
6. Matt 16:21–23.
7. References are numerous, but here are a few worth looking up: Rom 1:1–4; Phil 2:5–11; Col 1:15–20.

8. D. A. Carson, *When Jesus Confronts the World* (Grand Rapids, Mich.: Baker, 1987), p. 59.

9. Acts 4:12.

10. For a helpful survey see N. T. Wright, *Who Was Jesus?* (Grand Rapids, Mich.: Eerdmans, 1993).

11. See N. T. Wright, *Jesus and the Victory of God*; Philip Yancey, *The Jesus I Never Knew*; Steven Chalke, *The Lost Message of Jesus*; Brian McLaren, *The Secret Message of Jesus*; Rob Bell, *Velvet Elvis*.

12. Matt 1:1.

13. John 1:1–14.

14. John 1:1; 8:58; 12:44–45.

15. Acts 7:1–53; Heb 8–10.

Chapter 2: Christ among the Gods

1. Jack Straw, Leader of the House of Commons, was front-page news in the *Guardian* and the *Daily Telegraph* on 6 October 2006, and the issue escalated in the news for almost two weeks.

2. Dr Jonathan Sacks, *The Dignity of Difference* (London: Continuum International, 2003), p. 50.

3. John 14.

4. Acts 4:8–12; Col 1:15–20; Heb 1:1–4.

5. 1 Cor 1:23.

6. Mike Talbot address: "Presenting Christ Credibly." Evangelical Alliance UK Council, September 2005.

7. 1 Peter 3:15–16.

8. Luke 2:49.

9. Mark 1:11–12.

10. Mark 1:24–25. In fact Mark's gospel is renowned for its idea of Jesus' messianic secret.

11. Brian McLaren, *The Secret Message of Jesus* (Nashville: Nelson, 2006).

12. Acts 19:37.

13. Chris Wright, "Rehabilitating Evangelicalism as Good News: A Short Biblical Reflection." Presented to the Evangelical Alliance UK Council, September 2005.

14. Luke 4:18.

15. Matt 23:23.

16. Matt 1:18–21; John 1:14–18.

17. Rom 1:4.

Chapter 3: Rumours of Angels

1. Church of God Doctrinal Commitments, minutes 2002, p. 81.
2. See Peter Masters, *The Healing Epidemic* (London: Wakeman Trust, 1988).
3. For example, the idea that miracles disappeared with the apostles was discredited by Rev Martyn Lloyd-Jones: "We must assert," he said, "that it is a part of our whole position that we believe in the supernatural realm, and in a spiritual conflict." *What Is an Evangelical?* (London: Banner of Truth Trust, 1992), p. 81.
4. See Andrew Walker, *Restoring the Kingdom* (London: Hodder and Stoughton, 1988).
5. Evangelical Alliance Euston Statement, December 1994.
6. 2 Kings 13:14.
7. See Colin Whittaker, *Seven Pentecostal Pioneers* (Springfield, Mo.: Gospel Publishing House, 1985).
8. 1 Cor 2:1–16.
9. Acts 2:22.
10. Acts 2:14ff.
11. Lord Hastings, "Forum for Change," 6 January 2006, Regents Hall, London.
12. The Transformation movement emerged in the 1990s and saw significant episodes of relational and community transformation resulting from prayer.
13. Richard Fletcher, *The Conversion of Europe* (New York: HarperCollins, 1997), p. 45.
14. See Wes Richards, *An Examination of the Growth of the Global Holy Spirit Movement* (Brunel University, 2002), p. 28; Philip Jenkins, *The Next Christendom: The Coming of Global Christianity* (Oxford University Press, 2002); Daniel Boucher, *Transnational Evangelicalism* (Evangelical Alliance Wales, 2003).

Chapter 4: Christ the Conversationalist

1. 1 John 4:18.
2. See Mike Riddell, *Threshold of the Future* (London: SPCK, 1998), p. 82.
3. Luke 2:46–47.
4. Mark 15:34.
5. Jonah 4:11; Nah 3:19.

6. Joel Hunter is worth reading on this. *Right Wing, Wrong Bird* (Longwood, Fla: Distributed Church Press), p. 111.

7. Rob Bell, *Velvet Elvis* (Grand Rapids, Mich.: Zondervan, 2006), p. 11.

8. Meeting, London, 10 September 2006.

9. I have attempted a foundational approach waiting to be improved on! See *Hope, Respect and Trust* (Authentic Media, 2004).

10. See Anna Robbins' essay "Culture War" in David Hilborn, ed., *Movement for Change* (London: Paternoster Press, 2004).

11. Acts 26:28.

12. Interview with Stuart Murray-Williams, 27 July 2006. It's also worth reading his *Post-Christendom* (Authentic Media, 2004) and *Church After Christendom* (Paternoster Press, 2005).

Chapter 5: Rock Steady

1. John 19:5.

2. York Minster inauguration speech, 30 November 2005.

3. Interview with Bertil Ekstom (chair World Evangelical Alliance Missions Commission), Association of Evangelicals in Africa General Assembly, Entebbe, Uganda, 21 November 2006.

4. Rob Bell, *Velvet Elvis* (Grand Rapids, Mich.: Zondervan, 2006), p. 63.

5. Interview with Dr Tom Wright, Newcastle, UK, 26 July 2006.

6. Croatian professor Daniella Augustine made this point very powerfully at the International Pentecostal Symposium, Stuttgart, Germany, August 2003.

7. Interview with Luis Palau, London, 10 September 2006.

8. Interview with Bertil Ekstom, 21 November 2006.

9. Interview with Ndaba Mazabane in Israel, 3 December 2006. Ndaba is president of the Association of Evangelicals in Africa and chair of World Evangelical Alliance.

10. Roy Hattersley, "Faith Does Breed Charity," *Guardian*, 12 September 2005.

Chapter 6: What's in a Name?

1. Ian Randall, *For Such a Time* (Milton Keynes, England: Scripture Union, 1996), p. 172.

2. Mark 9:38–41.

3. Brian McLaren, *The Secret Message of Jesus* (Nashville: Nelson, 2006), p. 167.

4. Isa 58:6–10; Mic 6:8; James 1:27.
5. See Jim Wallis, *God's Politics*; Joel Hunter, *Right Wing, Wrong Bird*; and Tom Sine, *Cease Fire*, which all examine some of these issues in the US context.
6. "Case for Support," World Evangelical Alliance 2006.
7. David Bebbington, *Evangelicalism in Modern Britain: A History from the 1730s to the 1980s* (Grand Rapids, Mich.: Baker, 1992).
8. John Stott, *Evangelical Truth* (Downers Grove, Ill.: InterVarsity Press, 2005).

Chapter 7: A Good Time to Be Good (News)

1. Written response from Tony Campolo, 6 July 2006.
2. Interview with Stuart Murray-Williams, 27 July 2006.
3. Written response from Dr Peter Jenson, 30 June 2006.
4. These figures were presented at the AEA's 9th General Assembly, Entebbe, Uganda. 20–25 November 2006.
5. "Case for Support," World Evangelical Alliance 2006.
6. Philip Yancey, "A Quirky and Vibrant Mosaic," *Christianity Today*, June 2005.
7. Barna Group, "Who Qualifies as an Evangelical?" 18 January 2007, www.barna.org/FlexPage.aspx?Page=BarnaUpdate&BarnaUpdateID=263.
8. Alistair McGrath and Tom Wright both made this point very strongly in my interviews with them.
9. Interview with Stephen Holmes, 7 July 2006.
10. Quoted by Philip Yancey, "A Quirky and Vibrant Mosaic," *Christianity Today*, June 2005.
11. Alistair McGrath doubted that this word would gain widespread agreement. Interview 27 July 2006.
12. Interview with Geoff Tunnicliffe, Yad Hashmona, Israel, 2 December 2006.
13. Interview with Paul Masusu, Washington, D.C., June 2006. Paul is General Secretary, Evangelical Alliance Zambia.
14. Interview with Bertil Ekstrom, 21 November 2006.

Chapter 8: To the Left

1. See Clifford Longley, *Chosen People* (London: Hodder and Stoughton, 2003).
2. See Graham Dale, *God's Politicians* (London: HarperCollins, 2001), pp. 29–30.

3. Acts 11:26; 26:28.
4. Martyn Lloyd-Jones, *What Is an Evangelical?* (London: Banner of Truth Trust, 1992), p. 53.

Chapter 9: To the Right

1. In 1999, *An Evangelical Celebration* drew together scholars from the entire spectrum of evangelicals to endorse evangelical biblical identity. This was an indication that certain beliefs could no longer be assumed within evangelicalism.
2. Interview with Tom Wright, 26 July 2006.
3. Simon Manchester sermon, "Announcing the Receiver, Matt 25:31–46," St Helen's Bishopsgate, London, 2 July 2006.
4. *Daily Telegraph*, 17 January 2007.
5. Christ Wright, "Evangelicalism as Good News: A Short Biblical Reflection," EAUK Council, September 2006.

Chapter 10: To the Centre

1. John Stott's *Issues Facing Christians Today* (1984) was a ground-breaking book. A fourth edition was published by Zondervan in 2006.
2. Moses, Joseph, Daniel and Esther all had to live in palaces without selling out their faith. But each had to choose their battle.
3. Matt 10:16.
4. Philip Yancey, "A Quirky and Vibrant Mosaic," *Christianity Today*, June 2005.

Chapter 11: A Good News Afterthought

1. John 17.
2. Eph 4:1–6.
3. John 17:6–8.
4. Mark 1:15.
5. Acts 1:1–3.
6. John Fischer, "Learning to Cry for the Culture," *Christianity Today*, April 2007.
7. Mark 1:1.
8. "Case for Support," World Evangelical Alliance 2006.

Chapter 12: God's Gone Public

1. Interview with Alistair McGrath, 27 July 2006.

2. John Wolffe, "Historical Models of Evangelical Social Transformation," in *Movement for Change* (London: Paternoster Press, 2004), p. 36. Also see Clifford Hill, *The Wilberforce Connection* (Oxford: Monarch Books, 2004), p. 148.

3. Leon Hynson, "The Church and Social Transformation: An Ethics of the Spirit," *Wesleyan Theological Journal*, vol. 11, no. 1, spring 1976.

4. Mike Morris, Executive Director of EAUK, said this in an informal conversation in 2005, and we have incorporated it into our corporate plans.

5. 2 Cor 5:20.

6. Jim Wallis, *God's Politics* (San Francisco: HarperSanFrancisco, 2006), p. 7.

7. A point made well by Kathleen Heasman, *Evangelicals in Action* (London: G. Bles, 1962), and Clifford Hill, *The Wilberforce Connection* (Oxford: Monarch Books, 2004), p. 184.

8. Michael Horowitz, "How to Win Friends and Influence Culture," www.christianitytoday.com/ct/2005/009/30.71.html.

9. Micah Challenge has adopted Micah 6:8 as its biblical mandate. Do take time to look at the website (www.micahchallenge.org.) and sign the Micah Call.

Chapter 13: Towards Evangelical Citizens

1. Matt 28:19–20; Acts 1:8.

2. Miroslav Volf, "Soft Difference: Theological Reflections on the Relationship Between Church and Culture in 1 Peter," cited in *Not Evangelical Enough*, ed. Iain Taylor (London: Authentic Media, 2003), p. 55.

3. Acts 22:22–29.

4. Dan 6:4–5.

5. John 19:12.

6. *New International Dictionary of the Christian Church*, ed. J. D. Douglas (London: Paternoster Press, 1974), p. 747.

7. Charles Colson, *How Now Shall We Live?* (Wheaton, Ill.: Tyndale, 1999), p. 33.

8. Martin Robinson and Dwight Smith, *Invading Secular Space* (Grand Rapids, Mich.: Kregel, 2004), p. 73.

9. Jim Wallis, *God's Politics* (San Francisco: HarperSanFrancisco, 2006), p. xxvii.

10. Interview by Collin Hansen, "Nicholas Kristof on Evangelicals, China, and Human Rights," www.christianitytoday.com/ct/2006/september/17.23.html.

Chapter 14: In for the Long Haul

1. In his classic book *A History of British Evangelicalism*, David Bebbington defines evangelical identity as Bible centred, cross centred, conversionist and socially active.

2. Leon Hynson, "The Church and Social Transformation: An Ethics of the Spirit," *Wesleyan Theological Journal*, vol. 11, no. 1, spring 1976.

3. 1 Tim 2:1–4.

4. *Weekly Gleaner*, January 2007. This is the equivalent of forty people killed in London over the same period.

5. David Bebbington, "Evangelicals, Theology and Social Transformation," in *Movement for Change* (London: Paternoster Press, 2004), p. 19.

ABOUT THE AUTHOR

Joel Edwards has led the Evangelical Alliance in the UK since 1997. As an ordained minister in a major Caribbean denomination and as an honorary Canon of St Paul's Cathedral, he is a passionate advocate of both diversity and unity within the church at large.

Joel is keen for the church to be recognized as relevant in all areas of life and so serves on a number of faith, government and public agency advisory groups including chairing the Churches Media Council. Joel is committed to seeing long-term change for the world's poor and co-chairs the Micah Challenge International Council as part of his devotion to championing their cause.